1920 Diary

1920 Diary
Isaac Babel

Edited and with an Introduction
and Notes by Carol J. Avins
Translated by H.T. Willetts

Yale University Press
New Haven & London

Publication is made possible with the help of generous grants
from the Lucius N. Littauer Foundation and the University Research
Grants Committee of Northwestern University.

Designed by Nancy Ovedovitz and set in Berkeley Old Style type by
Tseng Information Systems. Printed in the United States of America by
Vail-Ballou Press, Binghamton, New York.

Library of Congress Cataloging-in-Publication Data
Babel', I. (Isaak), 1894–1940.
1920 Diary / Isaac Babel ; edited and with an introduction and notes by
Carol J. Avins ; translated by H.T. Willetts.
p. cm.
Translated from Russian.
Includes bibliographical references.
ISBN 0-300-05966-3
1. Babel', I. (Isaak), 1894—1941—Diaries.   2. Soviet Union—History
—Revolution, 1917–1921—Personal narratives, Russian.   3. Soviet
Union—History—Revolution, 1917–1921—Campaigns.   4. Authors,
Russian—20th century—Diaries.   5. Soldiers—Soviet Union—
Diaries.   I. Avins, Carol.   II. Willetts, H. T.   III. Title.
DK265.7.B28   1995
974.084'1'092—dc20   94-24535
                                                          CIP

10   9   8   7   6   5   4   3   2   1

Contents

Contents

Illustrations

Editor's Acknowledgments

MY GREATEST DEBT IS TO VIKTORIA SAGALOVA, WHO IN 1991 PRESENTED me with the first complete Russian edition of Babel's diary and introduced me to his widow, and who in the course of my work on Babel has served as a most valuable Moscow liaison. To Babel's widow, Antonina Nikolaevna Pirozhkova, I am grateful for the opportunity to examine the manuscript of the diary and to learn more about his experience in the years that followed. My thanks also to Galina Belaya for finding time to provide her insights into the diary's publication and significance. I must also express my appreciation to the editor and translator of the German edition of Babel's diary, Peter Urban, whom I have never met but from whose work I have benefited. Efraim Sicher, with whom I entered into correspondence late in the process of working on this edition, has generously shared his expertise and provided answers to a number of thorny questions.

Institutions whose assistance I am pleased to acknowledge include Northwestern University's Center for the Humanities, whose 1993 fellowship provided the time to work solely on the Babel diary. Further funding from the Northwestern University Research Grants Committee supported (among other things) the acquisition on microfilm of the army newspaper for which Babel wrote, *Krasnyi kavalerist*. A short-term travel grant from the International Research and Exchanges Board made possible an information-gathering trip to Moscow. John Hudson and Elizabeth Vanderleeuw's exceedingly patient and skilled preparation of the maps that accompany this edition was supported by the William and Mary Haas Fund of Northwestern University. Through the cooperation of Lucjan Dobroszycki and Eve Sicular at the YIVO Institute for Jewish Research, of Dr. Janusz Cisek at the Pilsudski Institute of America, of Dan Sharon at the Spertus Institute for Jewish Studies' Asher Library, and of the Northwestern University interlibrary loan staff, I was able to obtain the photographs that convey the world of the diary.

To my colleagues Tanya Tulchinsky, Marvin Kantor, Irwin Weil, and Michael Balinsky, my thanks for helping to sort out Russian, Yiddish, and Hebrew translation questions. Students John Kieselhorst and K. C. Butts ably assisted with library research. To Jonathan Brent of Yale University Press, thanks are due for supporting this project from the beginning. And to Rayman Solomon, for computer and many other forms of support, my final measure of gratitude.

Editor's Note on the Translation

THE TEXT OF THE DIARY IS THAT PRINTED IN ISAAK BABEL', *SOCHI-neniia* (Moscow: Khudozhestvennaia literatura, 1990), vol. 1, pp. 362–435. The original manuscript, which is in the archive of Antonina Nikolaevna Pirozhkova, was also consulted. As editor of this volume I contributed to the translation's final draft.

For the most part Babel's style and punctuation have been reproduced without alteration. The style is frequently elliptical and many sentences are long, with numerous phrases separated only by commas. Babel sometimes incorporates snatches of direct speech without specifying where a quotation begins; in some instances quotation marks have been added to make clear where Babel is inserting the words of others. In other cases, quotation marks have been used instead of dashes that are a Russian equivalent. Words appearing in languages other than Russian (Babel used bits of French, German, Hebrew, and Yiddish) are left in the original and glossed in the notes.

Abbreviations that have been amplified for the sake of clarity include those for Red Army ranks: instead of "brigade commander," for example, Babel uses the Russian equivalent of "brigcom." Titles have been capitalized to conform to standard English usage. Dates have also been written out (Babel's 15.9.20 is given in the translation as 15 September 1920), but otherwise the original datelines are retained. The translation follows Babel's practice of listing place before date up to the entry for 20 July, and date first in subsequent entries.

How to spell place names is among the thorniest issues encountered in translating Babel's diary. The towns and rivers in the border region in which the diary is set can be found on historical and contemporary maps spelled in a variety of ways. Many are called something slightly different, or are at least spelled differently, in Polish, Yiddish, and (transliterated) Russian and Ukrainian. Babel's usage is not a sufficient guide, since Russian does not differentiate between "g" and "h," or between such spellings as "cz" and "ch." Nor can one rely on a fixed boundary line, since the borderlands in 1920 were disputed territory and towns continually changed hands.

This edition opts for a mixed system, rendering in the Polish form places now located on the Polish side of the border, and transliterating the names of most other places (now in Ukraine) directly from Babel's Russian. Thus some place names end in the Polish "-ów" and others in the Russian "-ov"; the same correspondence holds for "sz" and "sh," "cz" and "ch," "c" and "ts." Place names not now in Poland that are clearly non-Russian in origin (Hoszcza, Radziwiłłów, and Grzymałówka, for example) are kept in Polish spelling rather than given in the transliterated Russian form. The number of such places increases as Babel moves west from Zhitomir, where the diary begins, across the pre–1914 Russian/Austro-Hungarian border toward Lvov (then occupied by Poland, now Ukrainian). This mixed system reflects the multinational nature of the region.

INTERNATIONAL BOUNDARIES, 1914   INTERNATIONAL BOUNDARIES, 1923

Poland in the era of the 1920 Polish-Soviet War (John Hudson and Elizabeth
Vanderleeuw; boundaries based on Paul Robert Magocsi, *Historical Atlas of East
Central Europe* [Seattle: University of Washington Press, 1993]).

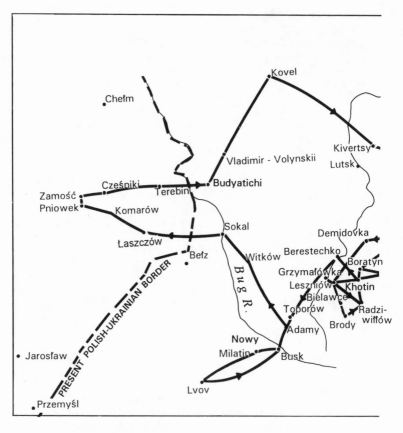

Babel's approximate route with the First Cavalry Army
(John Hudson and Elizabeth Vanderleeuw).

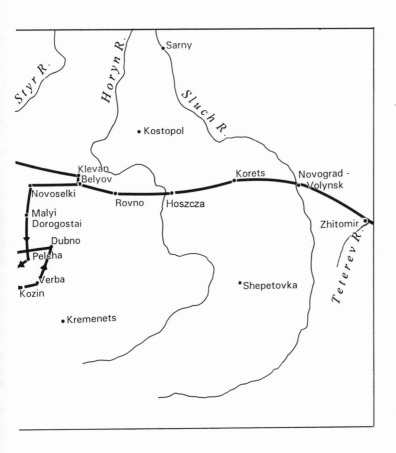

Introduction: Isaac Babel's "Red Cavalry" Diary

THE PROTOCOL DRAWN UP BY SECRET POLICE AGENTS AT THE TIME OF Isaac Babel's arrest on 15 May 1939 reads as follows: "1) various manuscripts—15 folders; 2) notebooks—11 items; 3) pads with notes—7 items." The confiscated writings included diaries, letters, and drafts of many stories—the fruits of intensive work during a decade in which Babel published little and silence was suspect. The writer (shot eight months later) never emerged from prison; those manuscripts (probably burned) never emerged from the files of what was then called the NKVD.[1] But not all of Babel's unpublished writing was lost, because not all of it was then in his possession. Some papers survived, as well as one diary, left long before at the home of a Kiev friend. The plain lined notebook had been filled by Babel nineteen years earlier during his service as a correspondent in the Polish-Soviet War. It has come to be known as the "Red Cavalry" diary, after the cycle of stories based on this experience that brought Babel instant fame in the 1920s and lasting regard as a literary master.

The diary lay in obscurity until the mid-1950s, when it came into the possession of the writer's widow.[2] Another thirty years passed before the advent of a climate in which all of it could be brought into print. In 1987, when censorship was in its waning days and revelations about Soviet history and culture filled the press, four major journals were approached with an offer to publish this piece of the past. They all refused. The refusal stemmed, in one case, from the fear that despite the loosening of constraints, the time had not yet arrived for publishing a document as sensitive as this; another editor cited the fear that the diary would damage Babel's reputation, implying that his treatment of the political and human landscape in the aftermath of revolution showed him to be too concerned with Jews. A fifth journal agreed to take excerpts—and thus, shortly before the end of the Soviet era, this unusual perspective on its beginnings came into public view.[3]

For those who know the stories, the diary provides both the thrill of seeing behind the scenes and a wealth of insights into Babel's artistry. Amateur and specialist alike can trace the path from observations recorded on the spot to the painstakingly crafted narratives of the *Red Cavalry* cycle. But it is in the intersecting spheres of personal history, Jewish history, and Polish and Russian history that the diary offers its most remarkable material. Readers unfamiliar with Babel's stories and uninterested in the transformation of notes into art will be caught up in two other dramas. In the foreground: a young man's struggle to define his relation to his Jewish identity, to the Bolshevik cause, and to the Cossacks with whom he fought for its victory. In the background, but powerfully affecting that primary drama: the struggle of civilians, particularly of the Jews among them, to weather the upheaval of this era of war and revolution.

Babel had made a mark as a penetrating observer of the postrevolutionary scene from the beginning. At the time of the Bolshevik Revolution in October 1917 he had been in Petrograd for about two years and had begun publishing stories and sketches that earned him the praise of Maxim Gorky, the premier literary figure among those who supported the Bolsheviks. Gorky, however, was profoundly disturbed by the direction of the new government in the months following the Revolution. The newspaper he edited, *Novaia zhizn'* (The new life), carried not only his critical commentaries but also the reportage of his young protégé. Babel's articles—a series of exposés documenting the gap between ideals and reality in 1918 Petrograd—were not uniformly negative. Babel was sensitive to the difficulty of bringing about rapid change and sympathetic to the regime's efforts to serve needy segments of the population. He was equally sympathetic, however, to the many casualties of this period of transition, from the premature infants whose mothers were too weak to nurse them, to the delinquent boys confined in an institution run like a corrupt prison rather than a school and refuge, to the starving animals in the zoo.[4] In July 1918, after seventeen of Babel's pieces had been published, the newspaper was shut down. The following year the twenty-five-year-old writer returned to his native Odessa, married, and took a job at the Ukrainian State Publishing House.

He did not, however, settle down—which was unsurprising, given his behavior of the previous few years. For since finishing at the Kiev Institute of Financial and Business Studies (where he studied from 1911 to 1915), Babel had accrued more than literary experience. The story goes (as related by Babel himself—not always a reliable source) that after publishing his early stories Gorky had told him he must go out into the world and learn something of life before he could realize his potential as a writer. That advice appears to have coincided with Babel's own inclinations. In late 1917 (though exempted from military service at the start of the World War), he served briefly as a volunteer on the Romanian front; in the summer of 1918 he went down the Volga on a grain-requisitioning expedition aimed at preventing starvation in the cities; in 1919 he joined Red Army troops fighting to hold back anti-Bolshevik forces advancing on Petrograd. Back in Odessa, Babel decided to embark on another risky venture. In the spring of 1920 he signed on as a correspondent with YugROSTA, the southern branch of the national wire service.[5] There is no doubt that he did this of his own volition or that he willingly accepted his assignment to the First Cavalry Army commanded by the already legendary Cossack general Semyon Budyonny.

Civil war was then in its third year. On one front after another, victory had fallen to the Reds. The Siberian capital of the White forces under Admiral Alexander Kolchak was taken in November 1919; by the following March the forces of General Anton Denikin had been defeated in the south. But another challenge to the victory of the Soviets was under way to the west, and now, in late April, developed into a full-scale war.

The sources of the Polish-Soviet War go back centuries, at least to the first partition of Poland in 1772, when it was carved up by Russia, Austro-Hungary, and Prussia. Newly constituted as an independent nation after World War I, Poland sought to take advantage of the nascent Soviet state's upheaval to expand eastward, restoring its 1772 borders and its former stature. This was not solely a territorial conflict—wars never are, given the powerful meanings that ideologues and simple people alike invest in real or imagined homelands. At issue on the ideological front of this war were two of the major forces in the post–World War I arena: communism and nationalism.

The Bolsheviks, believing that socialism could not succeed in only one country and that their revolution was the first of a series ready to erupt across Europe, sought to begin revolution's westward spread with the country that separated them from Marxism's place of origin. They saw their objectives in Poland not in nationalist but in internationalist terms, as a first stage in the eventual creation of an international alliance of workers and peasants. At Brest-Litovsk in March 1918, in the treaty that ended their war with Germany, the Soviets had insisted on the Polish right to self-determination; what they now meant by this, however, was the right of the Polish masses (who were to be aided by the Red Army) to overthrow their ruling class and join with Soviet Russia in making possible, first of all, a revolution in Germany.

Józef Piłsudski, leading the Poles, articulated the Polish mission both as a fulfillment of his country's historical destiny and as a crusade to save European civilization from the alien disease of Bolshevism.[6] In fearing the spread of Bolshevism the Poles were joined by the Allies, who had just fought to keep Europe safe for democracy. Winston Churchill, then secretary of war, was inclined to help the Poles but limited by the British Cabinet, which felt that France should take the lead. This the French did, extending credit for the purchase of armaments and also sending volunteers. (They included a young captain named Charles de Gaulle, just released from a German prisoner-of-war camp.) The United States, though as fearful as any country of communism (and undergoing its own era of Red scares), did no more than provide credit for the purchase by Poland of U.S. equipment left in France after the war. But there were American volunteers as well—pilots, who named their unit the Kosciuszko Squadron and flew missions supporting the Polish effort. Babel's encounter with one of those pilots, shot down by his division, forms one of the more curious vignettes in the diary. The American apparently tried to humor his captors and keep them talking. Babel writes (14 July) of their "endless conversation": "Whether he's just putting on an act or not, Mosher is frantically eager to find out what Bolshevism is all about."

Hostilities had begun in February 1919, in the wake of German withdrawal (after the November 1918 armistice) from the Polish-Russian borderlands. (The eastern side of the border was "Russian," of course, only in the imperial sense: the lands sought by Poland were Lithuanian, Belorussian, and Ukrainian.) The Poles quickly acquired the upper hand. In April they took Vilna; in August, Minsk. The Supreme Allied Council issued in Paris on 8 December a proposal for a provisional frontier (later to be known as the Curzon Line); diplomatic notes and negotiations were numerous in the months that followed. Polish troops kept moving, taking the Latvian city of Dvinsk in January 1920. But many accounts date the beginning of the war to April of that year, when Poland moved deep into the Ukraine. On 6 May the Polish Army (aided by Ukrainian nationalist troops) took Kiev from the Reds.

Occupation by a foreign power led the Soviets to appeal on

nationalist grounds for the support of all Russians, including those who had previously opposed them. This temporary shift of ideological emphasis from internationalist to nationalist is illustrated by the notice that appeared in *Pravda* on 28 May 1920 over the signature of archinternationalist Commissar of War Leon Trotsky: "Volunteers are needed! You, young men of the proletariat! You, conscientious peasants! All you in the intelligentsia who are honorable men! Russian officers, who have understood that the Red Army is saving the Freedom and Independence of the Russian nation! The Western Front calls you all."[7]

But action was not limited, of course, to calling for volunteers. It had been decided in March to move to the Polish front one of the most successful weapons in the Reds' arsenal, the First Cavalry Army—a force, as one historian versed in the parlance of cavalry puts it, of "16,000 active sabres."[8] This talk of cavalry may seem anachronistic, given the significant role of air power in World War I. But on the Polish side, as on the Russian, cavalry was the main offensive arm. The Russian Civil War—of which, from the Russian point of view, the Polish campaign was essentially a part—marked the last military reliance on cavalry in European history.

In Russia, cavalry meant Cossacks, of whom we see many sides in the pages of Babel's diary. Historically the Cossacks arose from disparate types—escaped serfs, wanderers, and adventurers, who as early as the fifteenth century had made their way south and east and begun to form communities in the lands separating the Polish and Muscovite states from the area controlled by the Ottoman Empire. Initially, given their independence, the Cossacks were regarded as a threat to stability; in time, however, they were co-opted by the tsarist government, which granted them privileges in exchange for military service. The Cossacks became loyal servants of the tsar, protecting the empire from both external and internal enemies.

Because of their connection to the tsarist regime, and because the Cossacks constituted a privileged estate with larger land allotments and a higher living standard than the non-Cossack peasants among whom they lived, most saw it in their interest to oppose the Bolsheviks in the Civil War. The First Cavalry Army was formed in November 1919 as part of the Red Army's effort to counter the Cossack forces siding with the Whites. Politically the *Konarmiia* (as it was called in Russian) was under the command of Stalin, then political commissar of the southern front, and its leaders were from Stalin's circle. (Their continuing closeness to Stalin is attested to by their longevity: Budyonny, the chief military officer, Iosif Voroshilov, the chief political officer, and Semyon Timoshenko, commander of the division with which Babel served, were the only military leaders with the rank of marshal to survive the purges of the 1930s.) [9]

If the leadership of the Konarmiia was firmly committed to the Bolshevik cause, the rank and file were for the most part less bound by ideological constraints. Some of Babel's notes reflect the independent mentality of the Cossacks (as well as stereotypes about their inherent predisposition to violence). "What sort of person is our Cossack?" he wrote on 21 July. "Many-layered: looting, reckless daring, professionalism, revolutionary spirit, bestial cruelty." That "revolutionary spirit" may have been harnessed by the Bolsheviks to serve their cause, but it had its own distinct roots. "This isn't a Marxist revolution," wrote Babel on 11 August, "it's a Cossack rebellion." And ten days later, with greater emphasis: "Our army is out to line its pockets, this isn't a revolution, it's a rebellion of Cossack wild men."

The reputation of Budyonny's Cossacks as a fierce and ruthless lot was widespread, and the Poles awaited their arrival with apprehension. One of the American pilots, later a chronicler of his volunteer squadron, described their approach as seen from the air: "Eight abreast, they trotted evenly along the dusty highway, each man carried an amazingly long saber hung not from his saddle but his belt-line, row after row of carbines hung aslant over their backs." The reaction at Polish headquarters to the news of the cavalry's advance is described by this writer in epic tones rife with the clichés of the day: "Budienny! This was the man who had been victorious in every battle he had entered, who with his hordes of half savage tribesmen, Cossacks and Mongols, had annihilated each of the White Russian armies. . . . The very presence of those wild Asiatic riders boded disaster."[10]

The First Cavalry Army, bombast aside, was not only made up of formidable horsemen; among its important units were the political departments of each division, which (as elsewhere in the Red Army) had among their responsibilities the education of soldiers and local civilians in the principles of the Soviet program.[11] As a correspondent for the army's daily newspaper, *Krasnyi kavalerist* (the *Red Cavalryman*), Babel was attached to the Political Section of the Sixth Division. (A city boy, short and bespectacled, he recorded on 12 July his first ride on horseback.) The term *war correspondent* conjures up romantic images, not all of which apply here, for Babel was not and could not be a war correspondent of the roving, unfettered type. The news agency for which he worked was a government entity, and the *Red Cavalryman* (four pages in most issues, with print runs of from 5,000 to 15,000) was a newspaper for the troops, full of inspirational exhortations and excerpts from official pronouncements. ("The Polish people are our friends and brothers" was a theme of a speech by Trotsky—now in his internationalist mode—featured on 4 July.)

There was a column for illiterate soldiers, whose literate comrades were urged to teach them how to read by studying such phrases as "Long live the leaders of the Revolution"; there were articles for those unversed in the fundamentals of ideology and philosophy ("Our Cognition of the Universe" was one series that ran in early August). The newspaper also taught fundamentals of hygiene and served the public health effort: articles entitled "What Is Typhus?" (2 September) and "What Is Cholera?" (3 September) remind us that the troops had forces to fear besides the Poles. Daily evidence of the multiple hazards of the front were the obituaries that appeared under the heading "For the Idea of Communism."

Red Cavalryman printed just four articles with Babel's byline— one eulogy for a fallen commander, two passionate accounts of atrocities committed by the Polish side, and a paean to the division's heroic nurses. It printed also, toward the end of the war, a letter of complaint from Babel to the editor that conveys the frustrating conditions under which he worked. "For the past month we have not seen a single newspaper," he wrote, "as for what is going on in the world at large, we have no idea. . . . I do not know whether my reports are getting through." (The letter and articles are printed in the Appendix.)

It seems probable that Babel wrote more for the paper than made it in. The young correspondent's other responsibilities, in any case, seem to have left him without a great deal of time for journalism. He was assigned the task of keeping a record of the division's military operations and called upon to write reports and assist the staff in other capacities. As the entry of 11 July indicates, the atmosphere at division headquarters (a misleadingly grandiose designation for whatever private house or public building had been commandeered in a given town) was tense at times. "It's an enormous job, positioning the brigades, there are no provisions," Babel writes. "Slender candles burning, divisional chief of staff in a cap, mopping his brow and dictating, dictating without a pause." But the mood was not always grim. Two days later Babel describes a scene that shows a startlingly blithe side of staff work ("handsome young clerks, young Russians on HQ staff sing[ing] arias from operettas") and suggests that while Cossacks did most of the fighting in this branch of the Red Army, they did not dominate its every aspect.

Some of the most painful episodes Babel experienced involved interrogating prisoners, another task in which he was sometimes called upon to participate. "We drag prisoners with us all the time, then hand them over to the authority of escort troops," he wrote on 30 August. Some did not make it that far, as it was not uncommon for the soldiers to murder prisoners without inquiries. Babel, who during battle performed support services such as assisting with field ambulances, witnessed this practice and tried on occasion to stop it. "The military commissar and I ride along the line begging the men not to massacre prisoners," he wrote on 18 August after one victory. In that same entry, which describes the drive to take Lvov, it is made clear that while he was usually on the sidelines, there was not always much distinction between the center of battle and the periphery. "The forest again," he continues, "bullets humming past, artillery fire drives us from place to place, nagging fear of aeroplanes, hurry up, it's about to explode, a nasty taste in the mouth, and you run."

Under these circumstances it is remarkable that he managed to do any writing of his own. Among the pages that never surfaced subsequently were some that, by Babel's account, had nothing to do with the war. "I am writing—a lot about pipes, about long-forgotten things, never mind the Revolution," he wrote on 12 August. The entries in his personal diary were made nearly daily, and in a great variety of settings—in homes where he was billeted, under trees during an hour's rest, and on the road, even during battle. A parenthetical note on 13 August reads: "I stopped writing here, two bombs exploded 100 paces away, dropped from an aeroplane." His twenty-sixth birthday (13 July), marked in quieter circumstances, found him reflecting on the distance separating him from home and from his goals, on the loss of some manuscripts on which he had been working, and on the consolation to be gained from filling a notebook, whether his personal diary or the journal of military operations—which apparently absorbed him as well. "I'm keeping my journal," he wrote as if encouraging himself, "that will be something interesting."

The military journal has not survived, and thus one cannot judge its level of interest or accuracy. As for the diary, it must be remembered that these entries enable us to know only those facets of Babel's experience that he chose to write down. To some degree the diary served for him the purpose that most personal records serve: it provided a confidant, a forum for sorting out feelings and impressions. Through Babel's notes we can track all the homely details of his weeks on the road—fevers, itches, cravings for comfort and tea. Drinking tea becomes a leitmotif—taking all the circumstances in which Babel managed to get a cup of tea would yield a cross section of his experiences. At one point his need for tea acquires the edge of dark comedy when, having made it to a billet after a grueling day, with tea about to be served, Babel and his companions must flee to escape the enemy. He records—self-conscious, as always, about his idiosyncracies: "We charge onto the bridge, milling hordes, we slip into the bog, wild panic, a dead man lying there, abandoned carts. . . . We move on, stop, sleep, stars. What I feel worst about in this whole business is the tea I was deprived of, feel so bad that it seems strange to me. I think about this all night, and hate war" (2 August).

Babel's notes swing from such intimate feelings and small details to the broad sweep of the enterprise in which he was engaged. His 22 August description of the brigade's routine illustrates the numbing and yet endlessly shocking scenes that became accepted as the norm. "Tired, shattered," he wrote. ". . . The system. Army stores and foraging parties give us nothing. Red troops arrive in a village, ransack the place, cook, stoves crackling all night, the householders' daughters have a hard time."

Recording these notes, Babel seems nearly always to have been aware of the end he meant them to serve: the fiction he would draw from them after the war was over. While the diary entries read like raw material by contrast with Babel's stories, they are not so raw as that term implies. Babel had precise ideas about what merited emphasis, and he was always alert to the aesthetic reso-nance of the grotesque detail and the potential for beauty amid horror. He was after not only incident but essence. "The day is over, I have seen death," he wrote on 1 August, "white roads, horses under the trees, sunrise and sunset. Above all—Budyonny's men, their horses, troop movements and war, grave, barefoot, spectral Galicians walking through the wheat fields." The entries are full of reminders (*describe, convey, remember*) to use or elaborate on par-ticular details, not always the most sensational. "For this day," he concludes the account of 3 August, in the course of which he had been under fire, witnessed rape and looting, gotten separated from his division, and tried to hitch a ride in a wagon that turned out to be full of dead bodies, "the main thing is to describe the Red Army men and the air."

Some of the writing is characterized by the sort of lyricism that here, as in Babel's fiction, is interwoven with reportage and laced with a kind of irony both subtle and brutal. One form of irony surfaces at times in the capsule portraits Babel sketched of individuals whose wartime lives were a world removed from the young writer's imagined version of their past. He was interested in getting beneath the surface, realizing that he could not grasp the experience of those around him without knowing elements of their prewar lives that lay beyond his field of vision. This is evident in the double-sided image he creates of an earthy nurse of the sort we see in *Red Cavalry:* "The nurse, she has served with Cheka [secret police] groups, very Russian, with her soft, bruised beauty. Has lived with all the commissars, I imagine, and suddenly—her Kostroma gymnasium album, the lady schoolteachers, idealistic hearts, the Romanov boarding school, Aunt Manya, skating" (31 July).

It is of critical importance to an understanding of the diary to recognize that Babel's own identity was deeply at variance with the persona he adopted during that summer. This was due not to the sort of natural metamorphosis that can be catalyzed by new circumstances but to a decision made back in Odessa. His family regarded his plan to go off to the front as suicidal.[12] Their fears presumably arose from more than the standard hazards of war. Of the unusually brutal violence of the Civil War years, a disproportionate amount was directed against Jews. It was a period of widespread anti-Semitic pogroms in Ukraine (most carried out by Ukrainian nationalist forces and by Cossacks fighting with the Whites, but with no side free of blame). Cossacks, whatever their present politics, bore the legacy of centuries of aggression toward the Jews. Poland, where Babel was headed, had its own wave of anti-Semitic violence in this period, starting with the proclamation of Polish independence in November 1918. It is not clear whose idea it was that Babel take the precaution of concealing his Jewishness, but it is clear that the name under which he left Odessa was not his own.

The papers prepared for him by the wire service bore instead of his obviously Jewish name one that could scarcely have been more Russian. It was a name suited to a warrior: Kirill Vasilievich Lyutov (the surname derives from the word meaning *ferocious*). This is the same name Babel gives the narrator of *Red Cavalry*—but in the stories the name is rarely used and only the most discerning reader will infer that the narrator is attempting at times to conceal his identity from his comrades. The diary, by contrast, deals extensively with—and derives much of its drama from—the practical and emotional consequences of Babel's subterfuge.

Seen historically, this self-protective wartime camouflage is an instance of what must be an ancient practice, one that no doubt continues in interethnic conflicts to this day. Some of the civilians Babel tried to fool were quite familiar with the phenomenon, for he had recent predecessors among Jewish soldiers serving in the Russian Army during World War I in the same region.[13] In Babel's case, the adoption of a Russian pseudonym should be understood as a temporary expedient rather than a rejection of his Jewishness. Neither before nor after did he attempt to hide or even deemphasize this side of his identity: it is prominent in his early writing as well as in his later works. That Jewish tradition was an important feature of his upbringing he made clear in the opening lines of the autobiographical sketch he wrote for publication in 1924: "On the insistence of my father I studied Hebrew, the Bible, and the Talmud until the age of sixteen."[14]

One curious reflection on Babel's actions of 1920 is his first story (published seven years earlier, when he was only nineteen), which deals in a condemnatory way with the matter of abandoning Judaism out of expedience. It is written from the point of view of the frail and senile old man whose name it bears, Old Shloime. The only thing to penetrate Shloime's consciousness in ages is the news of his son's plans to convert rather than be expelled from the town in which they both live. Shloime, though not at all religious, is horrified and, gathering his strength, hangs himself in the middle of the night, his father's Torah by his side. As in the final story of

Sholem Aleichem's "Tevye the Dairyman" stories, in which a daughter who had converted to Christianity rejoins her family when all the Jews are forced to leave their town, Babel's story (written at approximately the same time) shows how victimization can impel one to embrace one's identity all the more.[15]

All settlement restrictions on Jews had been abolished by the Provisional Government in March 1917. Jews in the Russian Empire universally supported the fall of tsarism, and a large number welcomed the Bolshevik Revolution that followed. The revolutionary movement of course included many Jews (some of whom had adopted and continued to use non-Jewish names—though this practice of taking noms de guerre in the underground was quite different from Babel's use of a pseudonym). In some respects it is odd that Babel attempted to hide his Jewishness, because there were so many in the Red Army who did not. (That captured American pilot, known to Babel as Mosher, is said to have given a false, Jewish-sounding name because of the belief on the Polish side that most Bolshevik commissars were Jews.)[16]

The *Red Cavalry* stories give the impression that Babel was the only Jew in Budyonny's army (the development of an intense contrast between the narrator's isolated self and a sea of Cossacks is part of the writer's design), but one learns from the diary that this was not the case. Babel refers on occasion to other Jews with whom he worked and, in the second entry, sharply distinguishes himself from the Party members among them. The opening of a Communist club in the field editorial office arouses this sarcastic assessment of the ideologically committed Jews for whom the war was but another stage in their service to the Revolution: "There you have it—the proletariat: these incredibly feeble Jewish men and women from the underground. Pathetic, fearsome tribe, march on."

It seems unlikely that Babel, alias Lyutov, succeeded entirely in hiding his Jewishness, from either the Jews or the Cossacks with whom he served. It was certainly known to some and possibly known to most, but not made an issue of. Babel appears to have played the game consistently among the Cossacks: when billeted with them in Jewish homes he took pains to keep his cover (although everyone involved may have known what was going on). On only one occasion (3 August) does a soldier label him a Jew—a stranger from another unit, who responds to Babel's request for a piece of bread by saying that he refuses to have anything to do with Jews. Babel may have expected that his use of a pseudonym would simplify his relations with the Cossacks, and perhaps it did. One suspects, however, that he did not foresee the degree to which pretending not to be a Jew would complicate his relations with the many civilians he encountered—specifically, with those large numbers of civilians who were themselves Jews.

The route traversed by Babel with the Red Cavalry led from Volhynia (one of the westernmost provinces of the former Pale of Settlement, along the Russian Empire's old border with Austria-Hungary) into the eastern part of newly Polish Galicia (part of Austria-Hungary until the Treaty of Versailles). The kind of warfare in which Budyonny's troops were engaged entailed considerable interaction with the local population in and around towns occupied by the Poles and Russians in turn—and a substantial part of that urban population, on both sides of the border, was made up of Jews. The diary entries are headed with place names that conjure up images of old-world Eastern European Jewish life: Zhitomir, Dubno, Brody, and smaller towns (*shtetl* is the Yiddish word, *mestechko* the Russian word used by Babel) with names reminiscent of Sholem Aleichem's Anatevka—Demidovka, Berestechko.

We may have clichéd images of these towns from the folklore of the shtetl, but it is important to realize that although some of the towns Babel passed through were tiny, many others were substantial, with long histories and prominent institutions, far removed from the muddy, ramshackle places of nostalgia-driven stage sets. Babel's 3 August description of the damage done to Brody (population about 11,000 in 1921) reminds us that these were urban settings, not villages. A prominent feature of the wartime townscape was "the Prague Bank building, stripped bare and vandalized, water closets, those tellers' windows, plate glass."

Nostalgia for the world of these towns is not solely a product of the complete destruction of their Jewish communities twenty years later. Emigration and sociopolitical change had made their mark by Babel's time, and nostalgia of a sort can be seen in contemporary depictions of the shtetl. Only a few months after Babel concluded this diary, in November-December 1920, Marc Chagall would paint a set of murals for the Yiddish State Theater in Moscow that emphasize the vibrancy and tradition of shtetl life (although, as in much of Chagall's work, the glow is tinged with melancholy). The inaugural production of that theater was an evening of Sholem Aleichem one-acters, heavy on stylized farce. (Solomon Mikhoels, who starred in this and many of the theater's other productions, was also the star of the 1925 silent film *Jewish Luck,* for which Babel wrote the titles.) [17]

Babel knew well the oscillation between tragedy and comedy that characterized the writing of Sholem Aleichem and much of Yiddish culture as a whole. In the teens he had already tried his hand at both a tragic depiction of shtetl life (in "Old Shloime") and a farcical one (in "Shabbos-Nachamu," a tale about the legendary trickster and picaro Hershele of Ostropol). In the summer of 1920 Babel (though, like the classic picaro, he bore a false identity) found himself a character in a wholly different kind of picaresque. The hidden truths and incongruities of farce were among its components, but the moments of humor one can find here are suffused with poignancy. For the most part, the reality Babel encountered as he traveled through the towns of Volhynia and Galicia was grim.

The region was just emerging from a devastating period of pogroms and wartime occupation when the Polish-Soviet fighting began. The historian Simon Dubnov, writing in September 1919, described the Ukrainian pogroms of the previous year as "a new fourth epoch of pogroms, carried out under the banner of anti-bolshevism. 'This song is not yet finished,'" he concluded, "and it will probably have a fearful epilogue." [18] What we see in Babel's diary is part of that epilogue. The belief that all Jews were Bolshevik sympathizers was one of the factors motivating the violence done to Jews in Poland, as in Ukraine. While this stereotype was far from true, many Jews, given their treatment by the Poles, did regard the Red Army as the lesser of two evils—like the old couple Babel met in early September who told him that it was "better to go hungry under the Bolsheviks than to eat fine bread under the Poles" (9 September). There were thousands of Jews who fought with the Poles, but one contemporary journalist points out that they did so despite the Polish Army's record. "When it is remembered that masses of Polish Jews enlisted in the army which massacred their co-religionists and raped their daughters," writes this observer, who supported neither side, "it will be understood how great is their patriotism."[19]

The Jews encountered by Babel were of course by definition in Russian-held territory, which no doubt tempered the views they espoused. Even factoring this in, it is clear that many genuinely welcomed the First Cavalry Army's advance. Their treatment by the Cossacks did not match their expectations. "Same old story," writes Babel on 11 July, "the Jews have been plundered, their bewilderment, they expected the Soviet regime to liberate them, and suddenly there were shrieks, whips cracking, shouts of 'dirty Yid.'" In late August, in the town of Sokal, Babel encountered a range of political orientations among the local Jews. There were a committed young Zionist; a pro-Soviet shoemaker ("a proletarian," writes Babel) disillusioned by the Soviet occupation; a beleaguered shopkeeper, his shelves emptied by looting Cossacks, who could not have had much love for either side; and, in the synagogue, Hasidic men and boys focused on the power politics of rabbinical dynasties. One figure who stands out among the philosophers and pragmatists in the diary is the most simple of idealists, a woman who makes speeches in her kitchen in favor of life being good (6 July). She is the female counterpart of the philosophizing tradesman Babel meets in the market in Zhitomir (the prototype of his character Gedali), who wishes for a benevolent state.

Babel knew the history that had shaped these positions and saw, as he traveled westward, physical evidence of the recent history that made people wish for a respite. "More and more frequently we come across trenches from the last war," he wrote on 18 July, "there's barbed wire everywhere, enough for fences for the next ten years or so, ruined villages, people everywhere trying to rebuild, but not very successfully, they have nothing, no building materials, no cement." What captured his imagination more, however, were the traces of the distant past in the landscape—a past with ample similarity to the present. "The Jewish cemetery outside Malin, hundreds of years old," he wrote on the same day ". . . it has seen Khmelnitsky, now Budyonny, . . . that whole story—Poles, Cossacks, Jews—is repeating itself with stunning exactitude, the only new element is communism." He saw history in the faces around him as well as in the stones. Kozin, 21 July: "Every house remains in my heart. Clusters of Jews. Their faces—this is the ghetto, and we are an ancient people, exhausted, but we still have some strength left. . . . An old Jew—I like talking with my own kind—they understand me."

That last line is of a sort one finds in a number of entries, but just as often there are expressions of the distance Babel felt between himself and the Jews of Volhynia and Galicia—so different, as he saw it, from the more assimilated, cosmopolitan Jews of his native Odessa. "These Jews are like portraits," he writes of those he saw in Kozin, "elongated, silent, long-bearded, not like our type, fat and jovial." It is a contrast of which he makes much in some of the stories of *Red Cavalry*. Here the contrast is more nuanced, the interaction between Babel and these Jews more complex. However kindred he may have felt them at times, his sense of their foreignness never left him. Certainly this was due in part to the uniform he wore and the masquerade in which he was engaged. It was due also to the fact that by late July, when Babel's brigade crossed the old border between the Russian and Austro-Hungarian empires, he was far enough west to be in a genuinely foreign place.

The entries leading up to this border crossing mark the growing distance from familiar territory. The increasingly multiethnic border region was a new world to the men of the cavalry, and to

Babel as well. "I am enchanted by what I see of the clean, whole-some, un-Russian way the Czechs live," he wrote on 12 July. A week later, remarking on the settlements of Czechs, Poles, and Germans through which they passed: "Different people, signs of prosperity, cleanliness, magnificent orchards, we eat unripe apples and pears, everyone wants to be billeted on the foreigners." It does not seem a region primed for socialism, but that same entry (18 July) illus-trates the Soviet claim of promoting indigenous socialism rather than imposing a foreign ideology by force. "An order comes from the Southwest Army Group," Babel records: "When we enter Gali-cia—the first time Soviet troops cross the frontier—we are to treat the population well. We are not entering a conquered country, the country belongs to the workers and peasants of Galicia, and to them alone, we are going there to help them establish Soviet rule."

When the crossing came they advanced across old trenches to the town of Leszniów and distributed leaflets about the establish-ment of Soviet Galicia. The distance between strategy and experi-ence, design and reality was on Babel's mind that night. "How unimaginably sad it is," he reflected, "these Galicians grown wild and pitiful, and the ruined synagogues, and this petty life against a background of fearful events, of which only feeble reflections reach us" (25 July).

In the days that followed, the division moved south along the Galician side of the border to the town of Brody. After the Rus-sian pogroms of 1881 Brody, given its position on the border, had served as a gathering point for Jewish emigrants headed from Rus-sia to America. What had been a haven was now, in the aftermath of the World War as well as of more recent fighting, in ruin.[20] Babel's sketch of the town (30 July) reveals the several senses in which he found it foreign, as well as the degree to which he distanced him-self from the Hasidic Jews and the once-prosperous Europeanized Jews alike. It reveals, too, the duality of his alienation from and identification with the Jewish community that recurs throughout the summer.

A reader sensitive to Babel's position can discern the multiple voices that here, as elsewhere, weave through his narrative. "These horrible markets, dwarves in gaberdines, gaberdines and peyes [sidelocks], old, old men," he writes, playing the outsider surveying the scene. A few lines below his voice shifts, as he expresses a link to these men that transcends all distinctions of type. Most of the city's synagogues are half destroyed; Babel looks over one of them with the caretaker and notes: "A fine synagogue, how fortunate that at least we have the old stones." He speaks of the old stones of the synagogue as a part of that collective to whom these markets of historical continuity are felt to be an inheritance. Both voices—that of the observer of alien customs and that of the member of the tribe—can be heard in the line that follows, as well as the voice of the writer thinking always of other words and forms adequate to what he sees: "This is a Jewish town, this is Galicia, describe it."

That synagogue caretaker would certainly have known he was speaking with a Jew; it is unlikely that Babel would have made any effort to hide it. (Nor does he appear to have curbed his propensity for poking around synagogues in town after town out of fear of being discovered by observers in his division. One entry— 9 September—even has him praying in a synagogue while a soldier walks around stealing all the light bulbs.) There were times, however, when he kept his cover among Jews, and not only as a self-protective measure when in the company of Cossacks.

The matter of Babel's selective concealment of his identity from other Jews is one of the most intriguing issues arising in the diary. No doubt he found it useful to be able to play both Jew and Russian (in Russian usage, the term *Russian* excluded Jews). There seems to have been something in him of the journalist's desire to adopt whatever guise would foster the unfolding of a scenario he wanted to observe. He dropped his cover under different circumstances for different reasons—sometimes to satisfy the questions of Jews who suspected the truth, sometimes to gain entrée to a Jewish milieu and thus satisfy his own nostalgia or curiosity. The first entry of the diary has him telling the young intellectual who takes him to

Sabbath prayers at the home of a Zhitomir tsaddik: "I'm Russian of course, mother Jewish, why?" He gave the same story two days later to a Jewish man harrassed by the Cossacks, seemingly as both an expression of solidarity and an explanation of his desire to be of help. "I go off to defend Uchenik," he writes. "I told them my mother was Jewish."

He changed his line as his instincts dictated: that half-truth represented a shift from the stance he had adopted earlier in his encounter with the family of that same unfortunate man. Welcoming him into their home for the night, the family pours out to him their story of being looted by the retreating Poles and advancing Russians in turn. A still-trembling little girl, sitting on her father's lap, interrupts to ask the uniformed visitor a poignantly relevant question: "Aren't you a Jew?" Babel records no answer, but he seems not to have given a truthful one. He does record his response to another question that hangs in the air: the question of what awaits the Jews under Soviet control. His summary: "I tell them everything will be all right, explain what the Revolution means, I talk on and on."

These words summarize not just what he said that night but also what he says on several similar occasions, particularly during the first half of the summer. Confronted by the accounts of victimized Jewish civilians, Babel at times maintains the fiction of his non-Jewishness and offers further fictions, stories that he privately calls "fairy tales" about the justice and well-being that will follow a Bolshevik victory. It was a form of consolation more than an expression of belief. Certainly he supported the goals of the Soviets and hoped that the violent means of revolution and war could yield beneficial ends. He believed, too, that better times lay ahead for the Jews. But the gulf between present evidence and long-term ideal was so wide as to make it seem impossible to remedy even the damage done by this war, much less the problems of centuries. "We are the vanguard," he writes on 21 July, "but of what? The population await their saviors, the Jews look for liberation—and in ride the Kuban Cossacks." And after another month on the road, again reflecting on what he has seen: "Along the way, on the cart, my thoughts, grief for the future of the Revolution" (23–24 August).

The spinner of utopian visions was a persona Babel adopted intermittently, not always in good conscience.[21] As the summer went on, his professed optimism was accompanied by a growing skepticism and by increasing discomfort with the ethics of consolation. His experience in Dubno provides a good illustration of how complex his role-playing could become. It was a split existence, in which a single day could entail a succession of roles. That day (23 July) found him in two Jewish households where (presumably in large part because of his Cossack companion) he hid his Jewishness, with a visit to a synagogue in between.

The volatile and womanizing Cossack Prishchepa takes him for an afternoon visit to a Jewish home in which Prishchepa is carrying on with the young wife behind the husband's back. Babel, in his Russian-war-correspondent mode, is stared at by the woman and pointedly asked his surname. "I'm in an idiotic position," he writes, "I stay quiet, limp, polite, say thank you for every move she makes." In response to the husband's question about whether small private businesses will be permitted under socialism, Babel answers in the affirmative and launches into what he cynically refers to as "my usual system": "miraculous things are happening in Russia— express trains, free food for children, theaters, the International. They listen with delight and disbelief. I think—you'll have your diamond-studded sky, everything and everyone will be turned upside down and inside out for the umpteenth time, and feel sorry for them."

If Babel dispensed facile and comforting visions, he sought for himself a different kind of comfort and a deeper understanding both of the Jewish history to which he belonged and of the revolutionary future he was helping to make. It is in this context that one must understand his account of a Dubno synagogue during the evening's Sabbath service. Sitting in the synagogue, he does not idealize what he sees. "Of all the Jews in Dubno the most repulsive looking seem to have gathered here," he writes of the "misshapen little figures" around him—and the aesthetic judgment he passes on the people finds an equivalent in his description of the setting. "There are no adornments in the building," he writes, "everything is white and plain to the point of asceticism, everything is fleshless, bloodless, to a grotesque degree, you have to have the soul of a Jew to sense what it means. But what does the soul consist of? Can it be that ours is the century in which they perish?"

His abstract musings about the nature of the Jewish soul and the effects on it of historical change may have been fueled by an experience during the next phase of the day, which requires a shift back into his Russian persona. In the home of the Jews with whom he and Prishchepa spend the night he is confronted by another sort of grotesque—one that cannot be reduced to abstraction. What he records is not his hosts' questions or their stories of abuse but a case of abuse he himself witnesses—minor, perhaps, but telling. His account is limited to one sentence from which we must extrapolate the scene. Prishchepa wants to be entertained with a musical performance; describing the Cossack's target, Babel writes: "the fat boy with the solid, dull-witted face, breathless with terror, says that he's not in the mood."

He notes nothing about what he did or said on this occasion. What he writes on the following day, however, shows him to be acutely aware of *himself* as a kind of performer, playing to the Jews as well as the Cossacks. He is aware, too, that he cannot assuage his conscience by maintaining that he is purely an observer rather than a participant in victimization. His experience the next day in the town of Demidovka shows this more sharply than any other. In Dubno, as elsewhere, he had found relief from subterfuge while in the synagogue ("A quiet evening in the synagogue," he wrote that evening, "that always has an irresistible effect on me."). But it was not always possible to take on and shed personas as the spirit dictated. In Demidovka, Babel finds himself pulled simultaneously toward his secular and his religious selves, for the home where he is billeted with Prishchepa is both a domestic setting and a place of prayer.

It is a day doubly sacred to this proud and pious Jewish family—the Sabbath and the eve of Tisha b'Av, a day of fasting to commemorate the destruction in ancient times of the First and Second Temples in Jerusalem. Babel knew the significance of the holiday and was troubled by his participation in yet another act of desecration. Prishchepa rages, demanding a meal; "I keep quiet," writes Babel later that evening, "because I'm a Russian." Privately appalled, he nonetheless eats too, then records in his diary: "We eat like oxen, fried potatoes and five tumblersful of coffee each. We sweat, they keep serving us, all this is terrible, I tell them fairy tales about Bolshevism—the blossoming, the express trains, Moscow's textile mills, universities, . . . I captivate all these tormented people."

His polished visions of the future yield to dark images of the past, as Babel's performance is followed by that of a young man who chants the liturgy traditional to the holiday. Babel may not have known the ritual well enough to identify the text (his notes toward a never-written story about this incident include the query "What do they read on Tisha b'Av?"),[22] but his years of study enabled him to understand the Hebrew words. The central reading for the evening service is Lamentations. In describing the gist and the setting, Babel draws the analogy between past and present that is traditionally drawn by Jews with each successive period of destruction: "The terrible words of the prophet—they eat dung, their maidens are ravished, their menfolk killed, Israel subjugated, words of wrath and sorrow. The lamp smokes, the old woman wails, the young man sings melodiously, girls in white stockings, outside—Demidovka, night, Cossacks, all just as it was when the Temple was destroyed."

In traditional practice the service does not end in despair. The recitation of Lamentations is followed by a series of dirges called *kinot,* which are not just outpourings of grief but also expressions of faith in redemption.[23] One text added to the kinot after the twelfth century, the poet Judah Halevi's "Ode to Zion," includes this vision of a reclaimed Holy Land: "The air of your land is the very life of the soul, the grains of your dust are flowing myrrh, your rivers are honey from the comb."[24] Babel writes that his listeners were enthralled by his tales of a paradisical Moscow. One wonders if they—or he—connected his promise of deliverance close at hand with the ancient rhetoric of Jerusalem restored.

The episode in Demidovka, which occurs about one-third of the way into the diary, is one of the central experiences Babel recounts and something of a turning point. What he writes two days later makes clear that his evening and morning in Demidovka occasioned some soul-searching. Settled in the town of Leszniów in another Jewish home ("prosperity, cleanliness, quiet, splendid coffee, clean children"), Babel reflects: "I feel anguished, I need to think about it all, Galicia, the world war, my own destiny" (26 July).

Part of what he needed to think about, as the next lines indicate, was his role within the army. The attempt to grasp the larger significance of events gives way to notes reminding himself to write also about the immediate, day-to-day issues that dominated his experience: "The life of our division. About Bakhturov, about the div. commander, about the Cossacks, the looting, the avant-garde of the avant-garde. I am an outsider."

Red Cavalry is largely a series of variations on the theme stated in that final sentence. Babel's outsider status with respect to the Cossacks is its primary meaning; his distance from the Jews of the war zone was of a different kind. One stark illustration of his distance from both can be found in the mid-August account of his entrance into the conquered town of Toporów. Writing the entry, Babel must have been conscious of describing the two sets of people in the scene before him, civilians and soldiers, in polar terms—broken and vibrant, black and red. The writer, though he rides with the Cossacks, is beyond the lens: "A dreadful, an eerie town, Jews in their doorways look like corpses, how much more can happen to you, I think, black beards, bent backs, ruined homes, . . . indescribable—that resigned, burning Jewish sadness. . . . The 2nd Brigade rides through. Topknots, clothes made out of rugs, red tobacco pouches, short carbines, their commanders on imposing horses, a Budyonny brigade. A ride-past, bands playing, greetings, sons of the Revolution" (18 August).

Babel's stories emphasize his longing for camaraderie with these exotic horsemen, despite the fact that their behavior horrified as well as enthralled him. The diary is heavier on horror, lighter on admiration—one does not see, as in the stories, the narrator's intermittent desire to remake himself in the Cossacks' image. Babel's ambivalence comes out in many places, including an episode that follows the evening prayers in Demidovka. He eavesdrops as his Cossack companion seduces a young woman in the household; she wavers, torn between resistance and submission, and Babel feels both dismayed by and sympathetic to her indecision. "She is in agonies," he writes, "who understands her soul better than I?" (24 July).

He sought intimacy with the Cossacks at times, deriving satisfaction from the contact. His stance is more that of the anthropologist than of the weakling intellectual who wishes he could shed his scruples. Some passages (like this one from 9 August) read like field notes: "They are all more or less peasants, in the evening they sing songs that sound like church music in lusty voices, their devotion to horses, beside each man a little heap—saddle, bridle, ornamented saber, greatcoat, I sleep in the midst of them. . . . The cavalry and its horses recuperate after their inhuman toil, men take a healing rest from cruelty, living together, singing quietly, telling each other stories."

Trying to expose all their dimensions, he was interested in what distinguished one subset and one individual from another. "At night I have Cossack visitors," he wrote two days later. "Incessant rain, they dry out and eat their supper in my room. The religious Cossack in the soft hat, pale face, fair moustache. They are serious, friendly, wild but somehow more attractive, more domesticated, less foul-mouthed, more peaceable than the Don Cossacks and those from Stavropol." His anthropological impulse is tempered at times when experience brings out the measure of truth in the stereotype of the savage Cossack. After a particularly vicious and grueling stretch of fighting that included the massacre of many prisoners, analytical description gives way to emotion, with Babel admitting that further analysis is beyond his strength: "I must look deeply into the soul of the fighting man, I am trying to, but it's all horrible, wild beasts with principles" (18 August).

That bestiality was not something he could regard as entirely external to himself. Grieved by his inclusion in a destructive force that moved "like a whirlwind, like a stream of lava, hated by everyone" (6 August), he sometimes uses the first-person plural in describing the troops' transgressions ("Our way of bringing freedom," he writes on 18 August "—horrible"). Nor does he leave out his own transgressions—minor in comparison with murder, but brutal nonetheless from the viewpoint of civilians. When the machine-gun buggy in which he is riding breaks down and it is up to him to get it repaired, the need to pull out of town ahead of the enemy overcomes any pangs of conscience he might have felt. "My scene with the smith, pushed a woman out of the way, shrieks and tears," he writes. ". . . I go through the whole arsenal, persuasion, threats, entreaties, a promise of sugar had most effect. A long story, one smith ill, I haul him round to another, more weeping and wailing, he is hauled off home again" (2 August).

The homeowners with whom troops were billeted were loath to share their stores of food with the occupying army. Babel records a few situations in which he pressured people to hand over what they were hoarding (none as extreme as in the story "Zamość," in which the narrator lights a match to the rushes on the floor when the landlady denies that there is anything to eat). The diary shows no evidence that Babel (unlike his narrator in "My First Goose)" was motivated by the desire to demonstrate to himself and the watching Cossacks that he was capable of the requisite ruthlessness. What it shows is that in a state of hunger and frustration he was capable of callousness. One entry captures that quality in a striking snapshot. It was the third of August; Babel was fresh from the battlefield near Brody ("the dreadful field, sown with mangled men, . . . naked young bodies gleaming white in the sun, jettisoned notebooks, leaflets, soldiers' books, Bibles, bodies amid the wheat"). Separated from his division, he tags onto another and rides with them into a town. "Five minutes after our arrival the looting starts," he records, "women struggling, weeping and wailing, it's unbearable, I can't stand these never-ending horrors, I go looking for a nurse, I feel unbearably sad, I pinch a mug of milk from the regimental commander, snatch a flat cake out of the hands of a peasant woman's little boy."

That little boy may remain on the reader's mind, along with the raped women and the other civilians violated by Polish and Russian troops alike. Incidents involving violence against Jews are particularly charged because of Babel's identification with the victims; from early August on, however, the diary gives increased attention to the Polish victims, both of this division and of the Russian troops that preceded it in the move north and west toward Warsaw. Along their route were desecrated Catholic churches and roadside shrines and estates abandoned by the gentry. Babel, always alert to otherness, was intrigued by what he saw of Polish culture and quick to draw conclusions about it (often falling into cliché). Billeted one night with a Polish peasant family, he writes: "The difference between Russians and Poles is striking. The Poles live a cleaner, gayer life, play with their children, beautiful icons, beautiful women" (29 August).

In Łaszków, as a fire consumed the barn of the village priest and soldiers tried to get around the proscription on looting, Babel stood watching with the priest and drew him into conversation. His ability to collect the stories of the most varied types is repeatedly evident in the diary; this is one of many times when he made use of that talent for engaging an interlocutor. His portrait of the priest (10 August) conveys both the man's mentality and the texture of his life in peacetime. And when there was no storyteller, Babel conjured one up out of the evidence left behind. In Berestechko, the priest had fled; Babel looks through his abandoned house. Photographs and books amply fuel his imagination, opening in it a new dimension. "How new all this is to me," he writes "—the books, the soul of a Catholic pater, a Jesuit, I try to capture the soul and heart of Tuzinkiewicz, and succeed" (7 August).

In abandoned manor houses, like the churches targets of looting,

Babel also entered into the lives of the owners via the mundane and exotic artifacts that remained. Farther northwest, now out of Galicia and within what had been Poland's pre–World War I borders, the troops came upon a grand estate abandoned in haste and vandalized by Russians who had come before. Babel's description of the interior is a still life gone awry: "Fine cut glass, . . . lady's dressing table, French novels on little tables, many French and Polish books on child care, intimate women's accoutrements all smashed, some butter left in a butter dish, newlyweds?" (29 August). The animals in the scene are not the lapdogs appropriate to the setting but muddy cavalry horses. It was raining, as it did for days on end in late August, and the troops had brought their horses into the drawing room. There they stood, juxtaposed with treasure—a chest of rare books ("Polish Code of Laws, precious bindings, 16th-century Polish manuscripts, monkish chronicles"). As the Cossacks set about damaging what was left, Babel's drive to observe and record what lay before him proved stronger than his revulsion at what he was seeing. "An unbearable feeling," he writes, "I want to run away from these vandals, but they walk around, searching, describe their gait, their faces, their hats, their foul language." Watching them, he was gathering his own booty.

His collection of images was enriched by his contact with the brigade and division commanders, on whom he frequently notes his thoughts. These observations are particularly pointed from early August, when he was alarmed by a shake-up in the division command, to early September, when the routing of the Red Army by the Poles created tension and recriminations. Tracing his notes on the new division commander, Apanasenko, one can see Babel's interest both in precise details and in the essence they reflect. On 5 August (after his first encounter with the new commander): "Remember—Apanasenko's figure, his face, his joyousness, his love of horses"; 11 August, after an interview: "Very interesting. This I must remember. His obtuse, terrible face, his powerful, stocky frame"; 18 August, in the course of what proved an unsuccessful effort to take eastern Galicia's largest city: "Information on Lvov's defenses—professors, women, adolescents. Apanasenko will massacre them, he hates the intelligentsia, and it goes deep, he wants a state of peasants and Cossacks, aristocratic in its own peculiar way."

The battle for Lvov was lost in the same week that, on the more important of the war's two fronts, other divisions of the Red Army were struggling to take Warsaw. The Soviets were preparing to enter the capital on 17 August; their defeat by Polish forces under General Władysław Sikorski, in what the Poles heralded as the Miracle on the Vistula, forced them to flee the following day. The Soviets' failure to achieve their principal objective (part of the context of the final despairing weeks of Babel's notes) is not mentioned in the diary. Indeed, there is much about the Polish-Soviet conflict and about the First Cavalry Army that one cannot learn from Babel's record alone. Budyonny, angered by the depiction of his troops in the stories of *Red Cavalry,* charged after reading them that Babel had hung around "with some unit deep in the rear."[25] The accusation that Babel had spent the whole war in a backwater, however, is contradicted by the fact that Budyonny and Voroshilov regarded his unit as strategically important enough to require their presence on a number of occasions.

The chance to observe the general and commissar up close further broadened Babel's palette. The analogy to painting was one he made himself. He first describes the two in a scene that has the range of one of those vast historical canvases populated by a hierarchy of actors. It is a multileveled tableau: ranks of soldiers moving in from the distance, the Soviet commanders balanced by the (temporarily conquered) antagonist, represented here by the stately home of an absent Polish count: "The wounded start coming in, bandages, bare bellies. . . . Budyonny and Voroshilov on the porch. Battle picture, the cavalry return, dust-stained, sweating, red-faced, no trace of excitement after their butcher's work, professionals, . . . nurses on horseback gallop by, an armored car. Opposite us Count Ledochowski's mansion, a white building overlooking a lake, not very high, not ostentatious, the essence of nobility" (19 July).

Like most historical paintings, this tableau does not contain the whole story. Babel moves a sentence later to a setting outside the picture, creating one of those juxtapositions that in his stories are so often calculated to foster irony and to expose what lies beneath the surface. The abrupt shift here from the public dimension to the private may be a function of chronology rather than design, but its effect on the reader is no less powerful for that. Babel, miserably ill with a high temperature, seeks civilian medical help. Commanders, counts, and Cossacks fade out; into focus comes the local medic ("a pathetic, good-looking young Jew, perhaps he was on the count's payroll"), gray with anxiety, who needs to know more than the story told by the "cavalry return" scene. He presses Babel for information about what is happening at the front and voices his own wishful view of what this Soviet victory means—that with the departure of the hated Poles "life will begin all over again." The diary does not record Babel's response, only his realist aside: "Cossacks, however, don't always behave well."

One last reading of an entry that encompasses the range of types and settings compressed into the diary brings us to the summer's final stage. On 28 August Babel's unit entered Komarów. Budyonny and Voroshilov arrive shortly after; the general watches in silence ("smiles, white teeth") while in front of the troops Voroshilov, riding agitatedly back and forth, bawls out the division commander for failing to engage the enemy. Cut from the town center, where military tactics arouse passion, to the civilian interior, where Babel learns the effect of a different sort of tactics: the pogrom carried out the previous day by Cossacks who had gone over to the Poles. The move for Babel, who walks from one scene to the other, is a descent into the abyss.

Komarów is the diary's nadir, the most gruesome scene he witnessed. The survivors tell their story, trying to make public the atrocities suffered by the town's Jews. Babel contributed to the publicity by writing a piece for the *Red Cavalryman* (see Appendix), in which he recounts the incident in gory detail and describes his horror as being a reaction shared by all his fellow soldiers. The article ends with an avenging battle cry that exhorts the troops to strike back at the savage dogs who could commit such base crimes. That rousing ending differs starkly from the despairing passage that concludes Babel's diary entry for the day. In the evening, resting in his lodgings, he has no kind words for the Soviet side, and not even the consolation of imagined revenge to offer. "The hatred is the same," he reflects, "the Cossacks just the same, the cruelty the same, it's nonsense to think one army is different from another. The life of these little towns. There's no salvation." What he goes on to say shows that he sensed the historical as well as the immediate significance of what he was seeing: "What a mighty and marvelous life of a nation existed here. The fate of Jewry. At our place in the evening, supper, tea, I sit and drink in the words of the Jew with the little beard, wistfully asking me whether it will be possible to trade."

Babel's lament for the loss of a culture recalls that of a character in one of his early stories ("The Nine," 1916), a Jew named Korb who has lived abroad, been wounded in the World War, and made his way, ill in mind and body, to Petrograd. His wanderings over, he turns to writing. The story depicts him visiting an editorial office in an effort to publish his life's work, a play entitled *The King of Israel*: "Korb wears an ancient, faded topcoat from his Antwerp days. His chin is covered with stubble, and in his eyes there is weariness, but also a fanatical look of determination. Korb has a headache, but he is writing a play and the first words of this play are: 'Toll the bells, for Judaea has perished.'"[26] Although Babel's treatment of the hapless Korb's enterprise was gently satirical, he found himself four years later recording similar sentiments without a trace of irony.

In the days following the brief Soviet occupation of Komarów (the Poles retook the town the day after Babel left) came the military low point: the defeat of Babel's division, along with the rest of the First Cavalry Army, near the towns of Zamość and Cześniki. The battle fought in the driving rain on 31 August (called by the Poles "The Battle of Komarów," by the Soviets "The Raid on Zamość") was the most dramatic Babel witnessed—a confrontation of the sort never seen in Europe again between two massed cavalry armies. The Poles charged; the Soviets fled. They escaped, but were left in a state of exhaustion. "Beginning of the end for the 1st Cavalry Army," wrote Babel on 1 September. "Talk of a retreat." That eastward retreat came: by 15 September, when the diary breaks off, Babel was back in Rovno, which he had passed through (heading westward) more than two months before.

Hostilities continued farther north, but the war was essentially over. Peace negotiations (which had begun in mid-August, when the Soviets seemed close to victory) resumed 21 September in Riga. An armistice was signed on 12 October, the peace treaty in March 1921. The borders it set, the product of a territorial compromise, were to stand until Soviet troops headed west once again eighteen years later. Their goals then—to win territory and export ideology—were the same, but on a far grander scale. (The Soviets had miscalculated about Germany in 1920, believing it ripe for revolution; in 1939, with not Soviet-style socialism but National Socialism in power, they miscalculated again. That September the Soviet Union annexed eastern Poland, which it ruled for nearly two years. When Germany broke the nonaggression pact by invading the Soviet Union in June 1941, the region described in Babel's diary was once again a battlefield.)

Armistice did not bring the demobilization of the First Cavalry Army: it was ordered to march to the last remaining front of the Civil War, the Crimea. (Along the way the Cossacks carried out a series of pogroms, for which a number of them were disciplined.) [27] Only two months of fighting remained before the Reds claimed complete victory. It is not clear exactly when Babel parted with the army, but by the end of the year he was home in Odessa, "completely exhausted, covered with vermin, and suffering from acute asthma." [28]

He stayed for a while in Odessa, working again in publishing, taking part in the literary life of the city (where he was already known and admired for his early stories), writing. An affectionate memoir by his friend and fellow writer Konstantin Paustovsky shows that the summer of 1921, spent with his family at a dacha outside the city, provided an idyllic antidote to the previous summer.[29] Later that year, seeking relief from his worsening asthma, Babel followed advice to leave Odessa for the mountains. He and his wife rented a house in the Caucasus, above the Georgian Black Sea resort of Batum. There he began turning the experience of the Polish campaign into fiction. He must have worked intensively: it was the most productive period of his life. During part of 1922–23 he moved to the Georgian capital (then called Tiflis), where he contributed articles to a newspaper; otherwise his assignments were his own. They were many and various. Between 1921 and 1925 he published the four stories known as the "Tales of Odessa," which celebrate the vitality and villainy of the Jewish underworld; two ostensibly autobiographical accounts of a child's experience during a 1905 pogrom, which express the grief of powerlessness and unfulfilled desire; and all of the thirty-four stories that made up the first edition of *Red Cavalry*. When Babel moved to Moscow in 1924, he was famous.

How the *Red Cavalry* stories differ from the diary could itself take up a book. They differ vastly, although some similar incidents and characters can be found in both. In a much-cited conversation with Paustovsky, Babel claimed to have no imagination—but though he may have felt unable (disinclined is perhaps more accurate) to invent whole worlds, he invented plenty, and he also turned his imagination to the shaping of forms.[30] Each incident, each portrait, is designed to particular effect, and the cycle as a whole is ordered so as to take the narrator—and the reader—through a process of growth from innocence to experience. It cannot be said that wisdom is achieved by the end, for while wisdom of various kinds is shown to be attainable, the impediments to exercising it are shown to be many.

The cycle is framed by two encounters with Jews roughly of Babel's generation: one (the young woman in the opening story who has seen her father murdered by the Poles) for whom no end could be great enough to justify her suffering, another (the title character of "The Rebbe's Son") willing to be martyred for the Soviet cause. The many nights Babel spent lodged in Jewish households are distilled in that first story, as are all the times he hid his Jewishness and felt the difficulty of doing so. That the narrator is a Jew pretending to be a non-Jew is hinted but not stated: by purposely withholding this fact Babel puts the reader in the position of those he encountered who were uninitiated into his secret.

Consumed by his own anxieties, the narrator stays aloof, but at the end of the story he is confronted by the young woman's anguished account of her father's death. All the stories of pogroms Babel had heard are summed up in the story's final lines: "'And now I should wish to know,' cried the woman with sudden and terrible violence, 'I should wish to know where in the whole world you could find another father like my father?'" The daughter's question is of course not so much a question as a cry of outrage. In the diary, when confronted with such suffering and with questions about what hope lies beyond it, Babel describes himself as offering comforting visions in response, particularly early in the summer. But in this story he makes the narrator speechless—both in the sense that the story ends before he has a chance to respond and in the sense that the question he is asked has no adequate answer. In the *Red Cavalry* stories no utopian visions—and no visions of the future at all—are presented, by the narrator or anyone else (with the exception of Gedali's wistful hope for an "International of good people" that he knows is an illusion). Perhaps because Babel himself grew so unsure of what answers could be adequate, he designs a narrator who, we are shown at the very outset, has no answers.

But others among his characters do, including the rebbe's son who believes so powerfully in the value of his sacrifice that he turns from civilian to combatant and leads a hopeless attack against the enemy. Babel may have drawn ideas for this figure from two incidents included in the diary, but the fictional product is wholly his invention. Identifying elements common to the diary and the stories is a rewarding game but one that has its limits, for there are many things in the stories that cannot be traced to the diary, and even more things in the diary that Babel chose not to use for his fiction.

"Stories Babel never wrote" is an intriguing topic that presents itself to those who read both the diary and *Red Cavalry*—and it could serve as the diary's subtitle. The diary contains material for a wealth of potential stories, some of which Babel planned but never completed.[31] There are many kinds of characters, especially Jewish types, whose experience is not reflected in Babel's fiction. Jewish life in western Ukraine and eastern Galicia, as depicted in *Red Cavalry,* seems moribund, the possibility of its continuation dim. The many Jewish settings we see in the diary—homes and street scenes in particular—amount to a different picture. There is much in it that is bleak, but there is an undercurrent of vitality as well.

In *Red Cavalry* we are told of the battle for Kovel, in the course of which Ilya the rebbe's son is wounded; he dies, surrounded by possessions from the two spheres of belief that defined him: Leninism on the one hand, Hebrew philosophy and poetry on the other. He is portrayed as one of the few true believers in either and as a rare example of someone committed to both. Babel's treatment of his death suggests that no one of his generation remains to carry on the tradition of Jewish learning and spiritual quest. The diary, however, takes us into Kovel, where we see that some degree of continuity is possible. "Quiet little houses," Babel writes, "meadows, Jewish back streets, a quiet life, wholesome, Jewish girls, youths, old men by the synagogue . . . Soviet power doesn't seem to have troubled the surface" (11 September).

That last observation is unique to Kovel, although we see elsewhere in the diary varied examples of the determination of Jews—not all of them quixotic—to pursue their ideals and carry on. Those that stand out include the committed young Zionist who shows Babel around the town of Sokal, the gymnasium students passionately arguing about history and theology, the besieged but dignified shopkeeper's daughter who, while Cossacks swarm over the shop, tries to behave "as if everything were normal, except that there are too many customers" (26 August). And finally, in the third entry from the end, that strong woman in a silk dress who takes Babel into her tidy house on Rosh Hashanah, shares with him her bread and butter, tells him about her husband in America—and moves him to tears.

A few days earlier, billeted with a Russian in the home of an elderly Jewish couple, Babel had remained aloof, eavesdropping on the family's conversations and noting in his diary, "They think I don't understand Yiddish" (8 September). On Rosh Hashanah, apparently impelled by the tie to his roots so evident in much of his writing, he goes off alone and sheds his disguise. Yiddish shifts from being a means of gathering material incognito to being a means of heartfelt communication, a medium of comfort. It is not clear in all the episodes involving civilians what language is being spoken, but when Babel writes of his encounter with this woman in the town of Kivertsy that "only language could help here," he seems to mean the Yiddish in which the two conversed at length and found common ground.

The incident brings to mind the autobiographical-seeming story of 1915, "Childhood. At Grandmother's," in which the boy narrator is nurtured by the food and stories of his Yiddish-speaking grandmother. The line of dialogue used as the title of the English translation, "You must know everything," is one of the grandmother's vehement admonitions to her charge. Moving this precept out of that context and into the context of Babel in 1920, one can see it as a guide to the experiences recounted in the diary. Babel did seek to learn everything possible about the people around him, and among his means to that end were the multiple languages he spoke. In the literal sense of the word *language,* he used Russian and Yiddish; in the figurative sense, he tried to master several more. Using each of these languages—of the Cossacks, of the commanders, of the committed troop-inspiring journalist, of the Jews loyal to quite different ideals and above all to their history—entailed allowing varying allegiances to come to the surface and others to recede. Part of the adventure of reading the diary lies in tracking the process of shifting identities and listening to Babel's voice as it modulates from one to another.

The year 1920 was not the last period in which Babel coped with concealing facets of his identity and playing multiple roles. His wife, sister, and mother emigrated to Europe in the mid-twenties; in the course of several long visits (after one of which his daughter Nathalie was born in Paris) he wrestled with the possibility of staying and remaking himself as an émigré. This he chose not to do, feeling strongly his tie to his career as a Soviet writer. He maintained an active correspondence with his family even as he began another family in Moscow in the thirties (to which there is no reference in his letters abroad). His life in the twenties and thirties makes a complex story, on both professional and personal levels. He participated (though idiosyncratically) in literary life; he wrote plays and screenplays, collaborating with Sergei Eisenstein; he translated and edited Sholem Aleichem and other Yiddish writers; he stayed in touch with comrades from the Polish campaign and used his military contacts in efforts to intervene for friends who were arrested; he worked for a time as secretary to a rural council, living on a stud farm; he wrote a series of daring stories about the collectivization of a village; he returned to the subject of the shtetls of the Pale in a novel (left unfinished) called "The Jewess," which brings one of those long-suffering matriarchs depicted in the diary to the promised land of the new Moscow; he maintained in the dangerous years of the late thirties a risky association with the wife of NKVD head N. I. Yezhov that was a factor leading to his arrest.[32]

The youthful desire for breadth of experience that we see in the 1920 diary can be found in Babel's life and writing of the nearly two decades that followed; so also can the youthful soul-searching about the multiple roles he felt called upon to play. The multivoiced narrative of the diary is suggestive not only of the nature of Babel's life in later years but, more broadly, of the experience of his generation. Other writers of Babel's generation, born in the 1890s and entering adulthood in a period of upheaval, experienced comparable searches, comparable calibrations and recalibrations of self. The young man who comes to life in the pages of this diary—anxious about the fate of the Revolution and of a larger histori-

cal scheme in which, by virtue of his heritage, he plays a role—
this young man so conflicted about revealing himself is a figure
revealing of his time.

Notes

1 For a detailed description of the secret police file documenting Babel's
arrest and imprisonment see Vitalii Shentalinskii, "'Proshu menia vyslu-
shat'. . . ' (Poslednie dni Babelia)," in *Vozvrashchenie* (Moscow: Sovetskii
pisatel', 1991), pp. 430–43.

2 Babel's widow, Antonina Nikolaevna Pirozhkova, was given the manuscript by the writer's friend T. O. Stakh, who had received it (along with
other papers) from another Kiev friend, M. Ia. Ovrutskaia. Pirozhkova sur-
mises that Babel might have left the papers with Ovrutskaia circa 1927,
when he closed up the Kiev home of his first wife's family after her father's
death and her mother's emigration. His own family had left their Odessa
home in 1924, when his father died and his mother and sister (soon to
emigrate) came to Moscow. (Interview with A. N. Pirozhkova, Moscow,
8 May 1993.)

3 The literary scholar Galina Belaya tells of her efforts to place the diary
with a publisher in her introduction to this first publication of extensive excerpts, entitled "'Nenavizhu voinu': Iz dnevnika 1920 goda Isaaka Babelia,"
in *Druzhba narodov*, 1989, no. 4, pp. 238–52, and no. 5, pp. 247–60. She
graciously supplied further details in an interview (Moscow, May 1993).
Fragmentary excerpts from the diary had been published earlier, in I. A.
Smirin, "Na puti k 'Konarmii' (Literaturnye iskaniia Babelia)," *Literaturnoe
nasledstvo* (Moscow: Nauka, 1965), pp. 467–82, and in Smirin's notes (pp.
497–98) to the drafts of stories published in the same volume. Selections
first appeared in English in Isaac Babel, *The Forgotten Prose*, ed. and trans.
Nicholas Stroud (Ann Arbor: Ardis, 1978), pp. 120–43. The complete text
of the diary was first published in Isaak Babel', *Sochineniia* (Moscow: Khudozhestvennaia literatura, 1990), vol. 1, pp. 362–435.

4 Most of the *Novaia zhizn'* articles (which appeared under the heading
"Diary") can be found in English in Babel, *Forgotten Prose*. All are reprinted
in Babel', *Sochineniia*.

5 On Babel's joining the staff of YugROSTA see V. Ia. Vakulenko's intro-
ductory note to I. E. Babel', "Novye materialy," *Znamia*, 1972, no. 6, p. 212.

On his work as a translator for the Cheka (predecessor of the KGB)—another of his experiences in Petrograd shortly after the Revolution—see Mikhail Skriabin and Leonard Gavrilov, *Svetit' mozhno—tol'ko sgoraia: Povest' o Moisee Uritskom* (Moscow: Politicheskaia literatura, 1987), pp. 306–10. Other biographical sources that have proved useful include Efraim Sicher, *Style and Structure in the Prose of Isaac Babel'* (Columbus, Ohio: Slavica, 1986), which has an extensive bibliography; Milton Ehre, *Isaac Babel* (Boston: Twayne, 1986); Judith Stora-Sandor, *Isaac Babel': L'homme et l'oeuvre* (Paris: Klincksieck, 1968); and Nathalie Babel's introduction to her *Isaac Babel: The Lonely Years, 1925–1939*, trans. Andrew R. MacAndrew and Max Hayward (New York: Farrar, Straus, 1964).

6 On Piłsudski's views, see Piotr S. Wandycz, *Soviet-Polish Relations, 1917–1921* (Cambridge: Harvard University Press, 1969), pp. 94–100 and *passim*. My other principal sources on the war are Norman Davies, *White Eagle, Red Star: The Polish-Soviet War, 1919–20* (London: MacDonald, 1972); Peter Kenez, *Civil War in South Russia, 1919–1920* (Berkeley: University of California Press, 1977); and Evan Mawdsley, *The Russian Civil War* (Boston: Allen and Unwin, 1987).

7 Quoted in Davies, *White Eagle, Red Star*, p. 141.

8 Davies, *White Eagle, Red Star*, p. 120.

9 Norman Davies, "Izaak Babel' 's 'Konarmiya' Stories, and the Polish-Soviet War," *Modern Language Review* 67, no. 4 (October 1972): 848.

10 Kenneth Malcolm Murray, *Wings over Poland: The Story of the 7th (Kosciuszko) Squadron of the Polish Air Service, 1919, 1920, 1921* (New York: D. Appleton, 1932), pp. 188–89.

11 On the workings of the Red Army political departments during this period, see Mark von Hagen, *Soldiers in the Proletarian Dictatorship: The Red Army and the Soviet Socialist State, 1917–1930* (Ithaca: Cornell University Press, 1990).

12 My source is the memoir by Babel's Odessa acquaintance Sergei Bondarin, "Prikosnovenie k cheloveku," *Vospominaniia o Babele*, ed. A. N. Pirozhkova and N. N. Iurgeneva (Moscow: Knizhnaia palata, 1989), p. 99.

13 An account of the behavior of these soldiers forms part of the documentary record compiled by S. Ansky (pseudonym of Solomon Rappoport) during World War I and entitled *The Destruction of Galicia: The Jewish Catastrophe in Poland, Galicia, and Bukovina, from a Diary, 1914–1917* (Vilna, Warsaw, New York, 1917). Translated excerpts from the Yiddish

text can be found—along with other works about this region in those years—in *The Literature of Destruction: Jewish Responses to Catastrophe,* ed. David G. Roskies (Philadelphia: Jewish Publication Society, 1988), pp. 210–26. Ansky's remarks on the behavior of Jewish soldiers serving in the Russian army toward Jewish civilians (then citizens of enemy Austria-Hungary) are of particular interest in relation to Babel's diary. There were some Jewish soldiers, especially among the military doctors, who tried to conceal their Jewishness. Others participated in abuses against local Jews, but Ansky writes of the majority: "Into an atmosphere of deepest despair the Jewish soldier brought to the population a certain moral support, and often material support as well" (p. 216).

14 Babel's "Avtobiografiia" appeared first in *Pisateli, avtobiografii i portrety sovremennykh prozaikov,* ed. Vladimir Lidin (Moscow, 1925). In English it can be found in *Lonely Years,* pp. xii–xiii.

15 "Staryi Shloime," Babel's first appearance in print, was published in the Kiev newspaper *Ogni,* 9 February 1913, pp. 3–4. It is printed in English in *Forgotten Babel,* pp. 17–21. For the idea of comparing the Babel and Sholem Aleichem stories I am indebted to David G. Roskies, *Against the Apocalypse: Responses to Catastrophe in Modern Jewish Culture* (Cambridge: Harvard University Press, 1984), p. 159.

16 Davies, "Babel''s 'Konarmiya' Stories," p. 853.

17 On Chagall's murals and their context see Benjamin Harshav, "Chagall: Postmodernism and Fictional Worlds in Painting," in *Marc Chagall and the Jewish Theater* (New York: Guggenheim Museum, 1992), pp. 15–63, and documents in that volume.

18 S. M. Dubnov, introduction to *Materialy dlia istorii antievreiskikh pogromov v Rossii,* ed. S. M. Dubnov and G. Ia. Krasnyi-Admoni (Petrograd: Komissiia dlia issledovaniia istorii antievreiskikh pogromov v Rossii, pri Evreiskom Istoriko-Etnograficheskom Obshchestve, 1919), vol. 1, p. xiii.

19 P. Ryss, "Between the Devil and the Deep Blue Sea," *The Jewish Tribune* (Paris), 1 October 1920, p. 4. The short-lived bimonthly newspaper, published (in Russian and English editions) by Russian Jewish émigrés and, as its masthead indicated, "dedicated to the interests of the Russian Jews," printed several penetrating articles about the political situation of the Jews in Poland. Of particular interest is E. Rabinovitch, "The Role of the Jews in the Struggle for the Border-lands," 1 July 1920, pp. 1–2.

20 The fate of Brody during its occupation by the Russian army at the

beginning of World War I, when Russian soldiers (Cossacks among them) dealt harshly with the Jewish population and set fire to much of the town, is recorded by S. Ansky in *Destruction of Galicia,* p. 211.

21 On this and some other points of interpretation my views are similar to those voiced by Alice Stone Nakhimovsky in her *Russian-Jewish Literature and Identity* (Baltimore: Johns Hopkins University Press, 1992), pp. 79–81.

22 Babel, notes headed "Demidovka," in "Iz planov i nabroskov k 'Konarmii,'" *Literaturnoe nasledstvo* 74, p. 496.

23 Roskies, *Against the Apocalypse,* p. 38, and see pp. 15–52 on interpretations over the centuries of the significance of Tisha b'Av and its paradigm of destruction. Roskies briefly discusses Babel's experience in Demidovka on pp. 136–37.

24 Halevi, "Ode to Zion," in *The Penguin Book of Hebrew Verse,* ed. T. Carmi (New York: Viking, 1981), p. 348.

25 "Open letter to Maxim Gorky from Semyon Budyonny," in N. Babel, *Lonely Years,* p. 385. First published in *Krasnaia gazeta,* 26 October 1928. Budyonny's initial diatribe against Babel's stories came four years earlier, in his article "Babizm Babelia iz 'Krasnoi novi,'" *Oktiabr',* 1924, no. 3, pp. 196–97.

26 Babel, "Deviat'," *Sochineniia,* vol. 1, p. 61. I quote from the translation by Max Hayward in Isaac Babel, *You Must Know Everything: Stories 1915–1937,* ed. Nathalie Babel (New York: Farrar, Straus, and Giroux, 1966), p. 24.

27 See Davies, *White Eagle, Red Star,* p. 232.

28 Nathalie Babel, introduction to *Lonely Years,* p. xviii.

29 Konstantin Paustovsky, "Rasskazy o Babele," in *Vospominaniia o Babele,* pp. 11–45.

30 Paustovsky, "Rasskazy o Babele," p. 27.

31 Some of Babel's fragmentary notes can be found in "Iz planov i nabroskov k 'Konarmii,'" *Literaturnoe nasledstvo* 74, pp. 490–99.

32 Yezhov was replaced as secret police chief in December 1938 (five months before Babel's arrest) and subsequently executed. His wife was a longtime friend of Babel's from Odessa. It was Yezhov's fall, not his influence, that probably figured in Babel's arrest.

1920 Diary

Zhitomir. 3 June [July] 1920

Morning in the train, came for tunic and boots. I'm sleeping with Zhukov, Topolnik, it's filthy, morning sun in my eyes, railroad-car filth. Lanky Zhukov, gluttonous Topolnik, the whole editorial team—unbelievably filthy fellows.

Revolting tea in borrowed mess tins. Letters home, packets for YugROSTA, interview with Pollak, operation to get control of Novograd, discipline in the Polish army is getting weaker, Polish White Guard literature, booklets of cigarette paper, matches, erstwhile (Ukrainian) Jews, commissars, all of it stupid, malicious, feeble, incompetent, and extraordinarily unconvincing. Mikhailov's extracts from Polish newspapers.

The kitchen on the train, fat soldiers with florid faces, gray souls, suffocating heat in the kitchen, kasha, midday, sweat, thick-legged washerwomen, phlegmatic creatures—lathes—describe the soldiers and the women, fat, overfed, sleepy.

Love in the kitchen.

After dinner to Zhitomir. White town, not sleepy, but battered, hushed. I look for traces of Polish culture. Women well-dressed, white stockings. Catholic church.

Bathe near Nuska in the Teterev, nasty little river, old Jewish men at the bathing place, their long skinny legs covered with gray hairs. Young Jews. Women washing clothes in the Teterev. A family—beautiful wife, husband carrying child.

Market in Zhitomir, old cobbler, blueing, whiting, shoelaces.

Synagogue buildings, ancient architecture, how deeply it all moves me.

Watch crystal 1,200 rubles. Market. A little Jew, a philosopher. Unimaginable shop—Dickens, brooms and golden slippers. His philosophy—they all say they're fighting for justice and they all loot. If only some government or other were a kind one. Remarkable words, little beard, we talk, tea and three apple tarts—750 rubles. Interesting old woman, sharp-tempered, shrewd, unhurried. How money-hungry they all are. Describe the market, baskets of cherries, interior of cookshop. Conversation with a Russian woman who came to borrow a washtub. Sweat, anemic tea, I'm beginning to get my teeth into life, farewell, dead men.

Podolsky, the son-in-law, half-starved intellectual, something about trade unions, service with Budyonny, "I'm Russian of course, mother Jewish, why?"

Zhitomir pogrom, organized by the Poles, continued, of course, by the Cossacks.

When our advance troops appeared the Poles entered the town, stayed for 3 days, there was a pogrom, they cut off beards, that's usual, assembled 45 Jews in the marketplace, led them to the slaughteryard, tortures, cut out tongues, wails heard all over the square. They set fire to 6 houses, I went to look at Koniuchowski's house on Cathedral Street, they machine-gunned those who tried to rescue people. The yardman, into whose arms a mother dropped a child from a burning window, was bayoneted, the priest put a ladder up against the back wall, they escaped that way.

Sabbath waning, we go from the father-in-law's to see the tsaddik. I didn't get his name. A staggering picture for me, though the signs of dying and complete decadence are plain to see. The tsaddik himself—his broad-shouldered, emaciated figure. His son—a noble boy in a gaberdine, I could see petit-bourgeois but spacious rooms. All very sedate, wife an ordinary Jewish woman, even a little "moderne."

The faces of the old Jews.

Conversations in the corner about rising prices.

I can't find my place in the prayerbook. Podolsky puts me right.

No candle—a tallow dip instead.

I feel happy, enormous faces, hooked noses, black beards with a sprinkling of gray, I think about many things, good-bye, dead men. The tsaddik's face, his nickel-rimmed pince-nez.

"Where are you from, young man?"

"From Odessa."

"How is life there?"

"People live."

"And here it's a horror."

A short conversation.

I leave feeling shaken.

Podolsky, pale and sad, gives me his address, a marvelous evening. I walk along, thinking about it all, quiet, alien streets. Kondratyev with a dark-haired Jewish woman, the poor commandant in his tall sheepskin hat, he never has any luck.

And then it's night, the train, painted over with communist slogans (contrast with what I saw among the old Jews).

The rattle of typewriters, our own generator, our own newspapers, a film showing, the train a blaze of light, its rumbling, fat-faced soldiers lining up for the washerwomen (a two-day wait).

Zhitomir. 4 June [July] 1920

Morning—packets to YugROSTA, report on the Zhitomir pogrom, one home, one to Oreshnikov, one to Narbut.

Reading Hamsun. Sobelman tells me the plot of his novel.

A new manuscript of Job, an old man who has lived for centuries, his disciples stole him away in order to fake a resurrection, a blasé foreigner, the Russian Revolution.

Schultz, that's the main thing, sensual pleasure, communism, pinching apples from landlords, Schultz talking, his bald patch, apples tucked in his shirt, communism, a Dostoevsky character, something in it, takes imagination, this unquenchable carnal lust, Schultz on the streets of Berdichev.

Khelemskaya, who has had pleurisy and diarrhea, has turned yellow, dirty shift, applesauce. What are you doing here, Khelemskaya? You ought to get married, husband in a technical office, engineer, abortion or first child, that's your life so far, your mother, you took a bath once a week, your love story, Khelemskaya, that's the way you should live, and you are adapting to the Revolution.

Opening of a Communist club in the editorial office. There you have it—the proletariat: these incredibly feeble Jewish men and women from the underground. Pathetic, fearsome tribe, march on. Then describe the concert, women singing Ukrainian songs.

Bathing in the Teterev. Kiperman, how we look for something to eat. What sort of person is Kiperman? What a fool I was, squandering my money. He sways like a reed, has a big nose, is nervous, possibly crazy, but he's a swindler, the way he keeps putting off repayments, manages the club. Describe his trousers, his nose, his deliberate way of speaking, how he was tortured in jail, a dreadful man, Kiperman.

Night on the boulevard. Chasing women. Four avenues, four stages: getting acquainted, chatting, awakening of desire, satisfaction of desire, the Teterev down below, an old medical assistant who says the commissars have everything, even wine, but he's well-disposed.

The Ukrainian editors and myself.

Guzhin, of whom Khelemskaya complained today, they're looking for something better.

I'm tired. And suddenly I'm lonely, life flows past me, and what does it mean.

Zhitomir. 5 June [July] 1920

Given boots and tunic on the train. Travel to Novograd at dawn, by car—a Thornycroft. All captured from Denikin. Saw dawn break over the yard of a monastery or school. Went to sleep in the car. Got to Novograd at 11 a.m. Went on in another Thornycroft. Detour bridge. Town more lively, ruins seem about the usual. I take my suitcase. HQ has left for Korets. One of the Jewish women has given birth, in the clinic, of course. A lanky hook-nosed man asks for a job, runs after me with the suitcase. I promised to come back tomorrow. Novograd is the same as Zwiahel.

On the truck are a soldier from a supply unit in a white sheepskin hat, a Jew and round-shouldered Morgan. We wait for Morgan while he's in the pharmacy, the poor devil has gonorrhea. The vehicle comes from Fastov. Two fat drivers. We fly along, a real Russian driver, shakes the guts out of us. The rye is ripening, hapless dispatch riders gallop past, huge dust-covered trucks, plump Polish fair-haired boys half-dressed, prisoners, Polish noses.

Korets, describe it, Jews outside a big building, yeshiva bocher in glasses, what are they talking about, old men with yellow beards, hunched traders, frail, lonely. I want to stay, but the telephonists are winding the cables in. Of course, HQ has moved out. We pick apples and cherries. Move on at furious speed. Then the driver, red sash, eats bread with fingers stained with lubricating oil. Before we've gone 6 versts the magneto is flooded. Repairs under a scorching sun, sweat, other drivers. I finish the journey on a hay cart (forgot—Artillery Inspector Timoshenko (?) inspecting guns at Korets. Our generals). Evening. Night. The park at Hoszcza. Zotov and HQ staff flash by, supply wagon behind them, the staff has left for Rovno, damn it all. Jews, I decide to stay with Duvid Uchenik, the soldiers try to talk me out of it, the Jews press me. I wash up, bliss, many Jews. Uchenik's brothers—twins? The wounded want to meet me. Healthy rogues, flesh wounds in the leg, walk unaided. Real tea, I have supper. Uchenik's children, a small but worldly-wise girl with squinty eyes, a trembling girl of 6, fat wife with gold teeth. They sit around me, anxiety fills the air. Uchenik tells me—the Poles pillaged, then the others descended, whooping and yelling, carried off everything, all his wife's things.

The little girl: aren't you a Jew? Uchenik sits watching me eat, the little girl on his lap, trembling. "She's frightened—cellars, shooting, then your side." I tell them everything will be all right, explain what the Revolution means, I talk on and on. "Things look bad for us, they mean to rob us, don't go to bed."

Night, streetlamp outside the window, a Hebrew grammar, my soul aches, hair freshly washed, fresh sadness. The tea makes me sweat. My support is Tsukerman, with a rifle. Radiotelegraphist. Soldiers outside, chasing people off to bed, sniggering. I eavesdrop: they suspect something, stay where you are, I'll mow you down.

The hunt for the woman prisoner. Stars, night over the town. The tall Cossack with an earring and a white-topped cap. They'd arrested Stasova's madwoman—a mattress, she beckoned to them, come on, I'll give you a bit—"if it had been me she'd have been at work all night, she'd have twisted and bucked all she liked but she wouldn't have run off." The soldiers chase everyone off to bed. They eat their supper—fried eggs, tea, roast meat, unimaginable coarseness, sprawling over the table—come on, woman, dish it up. Uchenik outside his house, they've posted a sentry, a comedy, go to bed, I can guard my own house. A terrible business with the madwoman they arrested. If they find her they'll kill her.

I can't sleep. I interfered, they said all is lost.

An oppressive night, an idiot with a piglet's body—the radio-telegraphist. Dirty nails and refined manners. Conversation about the Jewish question. Wounded man in a black shirt—wet behind the ears, a boor, the old Jews run about, the women have scattered. Nobody sleeps. Some girls out on the porch, some soldier sleeping on the couch.

Writing my diary. There's a lamp. The window looks out on a park, a wagon train goes by. Nobody is going to bed. A car drives up. Morgan is looking for a priest, I take him to the Jews.

The Horyn. Jewish men and old women on their porches. Hoszcza has been sacked, Hoszcza is cleaned out, Hoszcza is silent. A professional job. Whispering—they lifted everything and shed never a tear, real experts. The Horyn, a network of lakes and tributaries, evening light, the battle for Rovno took place here. Talking to the Jews, I feel kin to them, they think I'm Russian, and my soul is laid bare. We sit on the steep river bank. Peace and soft sighs behind my back. I go off to defend Uchenik. I told them my mother was Jewish, a story, Belaya Tserkov, the rabbi.

Rovno. 6 June [July] 1920

A troubled sleep, just a few hours. I wake up, sun shining, flies, a good bed, pink Jewish pillows, down. Soldiers tap-tapping with their crutches. Again—come on, woman, dish it up! Roast meat, sugar from a faceted wineglass, men lolling at the table, topknots hanging down, dressed ready to ride, red trousers, sheepskin hats, leg stumps jauntily dangling. The women run around with brick-red faces, not one of them has had any sleep. Duvid Uchenik is pale, wearing a waistcoat. Says to me: don't leave while they're still here. A wagon comes to pick them up. Sunshine, the park opposite, the wagon is waiting, they're off. It's over. Saved.

The car arrived last night. At 1 p.m. we leave Hoszcza for Rovno. The Horyn sparkles in the sun. I go for a morning walk. It turns out the mistress of the house did not spend the night at home, the maidservant and her girlfriends sat up all night till daybreak with the soldiers who wanted to rape her, she kept feeding them apples, decorous conversation, we're sick of fighting, we want to get married, go and get some sleep. The little girl with the squint became talkative, Duvid put on his waistcoat, his tallis, prayed with dignity, gave thanks, flour in the kitchen, they're kneading dough, they've set to work, the maidservant is thicklegged, barefooted, a fat Jewess with a soft bosom tidies up and tells endless stories. The woman of the house goes on about how she just wants everything to be all right. The house comes to life again.

I go to Rovno in the Thornycroft. Two dead horses. Ruined bridges, the car on a wooden platform, everything is breaking down, endless columns of supply wagons, traffic jams, men swearing, describe the wagon train held up at the broken bridge at noon, horsemen, trucks, two-wheelers with ammunition. Our truck rushes along furiously, though it's falling to pieces, dust.

Eight versts short, it stopped. Cherries, I sleep, sweating in the sun. Kuzitsky, a comic figure, tells your fortune in a twinkling, lays the cards out, a medical assistant from Borodianitsy, women paid him in kind for treatment, with roast chicken or their persons, worries the whole time whether the commandant of the field hospital will let him go, shows me his genuine wounds, limps when he gets up to go, left a girl down the road, forty versts from Zhitomir, she told him to go, said the divisional chief of staff was courting her.

Loses his whip, sits there half-naked, jabbering, lying shamelessly, photograph of his brother, a former staff captain in the cavalry, now a divisional commander, married to a Polish princess, shot by Denikin's troops.

I'm a doctor.

In Rovno. Dust, dusty molten gold flows over dreary little houses.

A brigade marches through, Zotov at the window, the inhabitants of Rovno, how the Cossacks look, an amazingly calm and self-assured army. Jewish girls and youths watch enthralled, old Jews look on indifferently. Convey Rovno air, badly shaken up, unstable, but life goes on, and there are Polish signboards.

Describe the evening.

The Khasts, a sly, dark-haired girl from Warsaw takes me, a medical orderly, malicious verbal stench, flirtatiousness, "You'll eat with us," I wash myself in the passage, all very awkward, bliss, I'm dirty and sweaty, then hot tea with my own sugar.

Describe this Khast, a complicated fury, intolerable voice, they think I don't understand Yiddish, quarrel incessantly, animal fear, the father—"not a simple matter," a smiling medical assistant, treats people for gonorrhea (?), smiles, lies low, but seems hot-tempered, the mother: we're intellectuals, we have nothing, and he's a medical assistant, a working man, so let them come, only quietly, we're tired to death, a mind-boggling phenomenon—the round son with a sly, idiotic smile behind the lenses of his round glasses, the ingratiating talk, they cater to me, a whole crowd of sisters, they're all scum (?). A dentist, grandson or something, they all talk to him in the same whining, hysterical way as to the old people, some young Jews arrive, people from Rovno with flat faces yellow with fear and fishy eyes, tell us about Polish outrages, show their passports, there was a solemn decree annexing Volhynia as well to Poland. I find myself thinking of Polish culture, Sienkiewicz, their women, Poland as a great power, they were born too late, class consciousness rules now.

I hand over my laundry to be washed. Drink tea incessantly and sweat like an animal, and look at the Khasts closely, unblinkingly. Spend the night on the sofa. Undress for the first time since we set

out. They close all the shutters, the electric light is on, it's terribly
stuffy, there are so many people sleeping there, stories about looting
by Budyonny's troops, fear and trembling, horses snorting outside
the window, wagon trains rolling down School Street, night,

TWENTY-ONE PAGES ARE MISSING FROM THE
MANUSCRIPT AT THIS POINT.

Belyov. 11 July 1920

Spent the night with soldiers of HQ Squadron, in the hay.
Slept badly, thought about the manuscripts. Homesickness, flag-
ging energy, I know I shall overcome it, but when? Think about
the Khasts, those nits, I remember everything, their malodorous
souls, their sheep's eyes, their startlingly high, squeaky voices, the
smiling father. Above all—that smile, his irateness, all the secrets,
the evil-smelling recollections of past scandals. A tremendous character, the mother, she's malicious, cowardly, gluttonous, revolting,
her lingering, expectant gaze. The daughter's revolting, elaborate
lies, the son's laughing eyes behind his glasses.

I roam around the village. Go to Klevan, a town taken yesterday
by 3rd Cavalry Brigade of 6th Division. Our patrols lined up along
the highway from Rovno to Lutsk. Lutsk is being evacuated. From
the 8th to the 12th there was heavy fighting, Dundich was killed,
also Shchadilov, commander of the 36th Regiment, many horses
killed, we shall know the details tomorrow.

Budyonny's orders about our loss of Rovno, about the incredible
weariness of the troops, the fact that furious attacks by our brigades
do not yield the same results as before, uninterrupted fighting since
27 May, if we aren't given a breathing space the army will become
unfit to fight.

Maybe orders like this are premature? No, they make sense, they
wake up the rear—Klevan. Burial of six or seven Red Army men.
Went for a tachanka. Funeral march, then on the way back from the

cemetery a bravura marching song, no funeral procession in sight. Carpenter—a bearded Jew—runs around the town, he's knocking together coffins.

Here too the main street is Schossowa.

My first requisition—a notebook. The synagogue caretaker Menashe accompanies me. I eat at Mudrik's, same old story, the Jews have been plundered, their bewilderment, they expected the Soviet regime to liberate them, and suddenly there were shrieks, whips cracking, shouts of "dirty Yid." I was besieged by a whole circle of them. I tell them about the note to Wilson, the labor armies, the little Jews listen, knowing and sympathetic smiles, a Jew in white trousers who had come to the pine forest for his health wants to go home. Jews sit on the mounds of hardened earth outside their houses, young girls and old men, it's dead quiet, hot, dusty, a peasant (Parfentii Melnik, the same man who had done his military service in Elizavetpol) complains that his horse is swollen with milk, they separated her from her foal, depressed, the manuscripts, the manuscripts, that's what makes me sick at heart.

Colonel Gorov elected headman by the villagers, 60 years old, an aristocratic rat from pre-Reform times. We talk about the army, about Brusilov—if Brusilov took the field what should we think. Gray moustache, mumbles toothlessly, a figure from the past, smokes home-grown tobacco, lives in the administration building, I'm sorry for the old man.

The clerk to the district administration, a handsome Ukrainian, exemplary order, retrained in Polish, shows me the books, statistics for the district—18,600 people, 800 of them Poles, these wanted union with Poland, solemn declaration on unification with the Polish state.

This clerk is also a pre-Reform character, wears velvet trousers, speaks with a Ukrainian accent, affected by the new times, little moustache.

Klevan, its roads, its streets, the peasants and communism far apart.

Hop-growing, many seed-beds, quadrilateral green walls, a difficult crop.

The colonel has blue eyes, the clerk a silky moustache.

Night, staff work at Belyov. Who and what is Zholnarkevich? A Pole? His feelings? Touching friendship of two brothers, Konstantin and Mikhailo. Zholnarkevich is an old hand, meticulous, able to work hard with overstraining himself, energetic without fuss, Polish moustache, thin Polish legs. The staff is Zholnarkevich plus three clerks who get exhausted by nightfall.

It's an enormous job, positioning the brigades, there are no provisions, the main thing—the operational sectors—is handled inconspicuously. Dispatch riders asleep on the ground at HQ. Slender candles burning, divisional chief of staff in a cap, mopping his brow and dictating, dictating without a pause operational reports, orders, to the artillery division, to army field HQ, we are continuing to advance on Lutsk.

Night, I sleep on hay beside Lepin, a Latvian, horses that have slipped their tethers wander around, pluck hay from under my head.

Belyov. 12 July 1920

In the morning, began my journal of military operations, analyzed operational reports. This journal will be an interesting bit of work.

After eating I ride Sokolov's horse. (Sokolov, a dispatch rider, has recurrent typhus, lies on the ground near me in a leather jacket, a lean thoroughbred holding a whip in his emaciated hand, walked out of the hospital, they weren't giving him anything to eat, and he was bored, he was lying there sick, drenched through, during that terrible night of the withdrawal from Rovno, a lanky man, unsteady on his feet, talks to the people of the house, inquisitively, but dictatorially, as if all peasants were his enemies). Szpaków, a Czech colony. A prosperous part of the world, lots of oats and wheat, I ride through the villages of Peresonnitsa, Miłostów, Ploski, Szpaków. They grow flax for linseed oil, and a lot of buckwheat.

Prosperous villages, midday heat, dusty roads, translucent sky without a single cloud, horse lazy, touch of the whip to make it run. My first ride on horseback. At Miłostów I pick up a cart from Szpaków go to fetch a tachanka and horses, with a written order from divisional HQ.

My heart melts. I am enchanted by what I see of the clean, wholesome, un-Russian way the Czechs live. A good headman, horsemen galloping in all direction, new demands all the time, forty carloads of hay, ten pigs, the Requisitioning Committee's agents want bread grain, the headman is given a receipt to say we've got the oats, thank you. Officer in charge of reconnaissance, 34th Regiment.

Solidly built cottages sparkle in the sun, tiled roofs, iron, stone, apple trees, stone schoolhouse, semiurban women, bright-colored aprons. We go to see Yuripov, the miller, the richest and most cultured of them, tall, handsome, a typical Czech with a Western European moustache. Splendid yard, dovecot—that moves me— new milling machinery, bygone prosperity, white walls, a capacious yard, one-story house, light and spacious, nice room, probably has a nice family, this Czech, father a poor stringy old fellow, all good people, sturdy son with gold teeth, well-built and broadshouldered. Probably a nice young wife and children.

The mill has, of course, been modernized.

The Czech has receipts coming out of his ears. We took four of his horses, gave him receipts in the name of the Rovno District Commissariat, took his phaeton and gave him a broken-down buggy instead, three receipts for flour and oats.

A brigade arrives, red flags, a powerful, well-knit body of men, confident commanders, calm and experienced eyes of topknotted Cossack fighting men, dust, silence, order, brass band, they trickle away to their billets, the brigade commander calls out to me: don't take anything from here, this district is ours. The Czech anxiously watches the smart young brigade commander bustling around in the distance, chats with me politely, presents me with the broken-down buggy, but it falls to pieces. I don't exert myself. We go to a second house, a third. The headman shows me where I can get things. The old man really does have a carriage, his son whispers in my ear, says it's broken, the front is no good, I think—you've got a sweetheart, or else you all ride to church in it on Sundays, it's hot, I feel lazy, sorry for them, with all those horsemen rummaging around, that's what freedom looks like at first sight. I took nothing, although I could have, I'll never be a real Budyonny man.

Back again, evening, they've caught a Pole hiding in the rye, hunted him down like a animal, broad fields, crimson sun, golden mist, the crops sway in the breeze, people driving cattle home in the village, pink dusty roads, from the edges of pearly clouds— flaming tongues, orange flame, of an unusual gentle shape, the carts raise dust.

I work at HQ (the horse galloped well), go to bed next to Lepin. He is Latvian, with a blunt piggy snout, glasses, seems good-natured. A General Staff man.

Makes stupid, irrelevant jokes. When are you going to die, woman, and grabs hold of her.

No kerosene at HQ. He says—we're striving toward the light, but we have no lighting, I'll go and play with the village girls, holds his hand out straight, doesn't lower it, strained look on his ugly mug, piggy lip trembles, glasses wobble.

Belyov. 13 July 1920

My birthday. I'm 26. Think about home, about my work, my life is flying by. No manuscripts. A dull misery, must get the better of it. I'm keeping my journal, that will be something interesting.

Handsome young clerks, young Russians on HQ staff sing arias from operettas, they're a bit spoiled by working at HQ. Describe the dispatch rider, those working for the divisional chief of staff, and the rest of them—Cherkashin, Tarasov, looters, lickspittles, syco-phants, gluttons, idlers. The legacy of the past, they know who's master.

Staff work at Belyov. A smoothly running machine, excellent chief of staff, mechanical work, and a real live man. They discovered he's a Pole, discharged him, he was brought back on the divisional commander's insistence, liked by everybody, gets on well with the divisional commander, how does he feel about it all? He's no communist, he's a Pole, yet he serves as loyally as any yard dog, work it out if you can.

About our operations.

Position of our units.

The advance on Lutsk.

Composition of the division brigade commanders.

Routine HQ procedure—directive, issue order, then operational report, then field intelligence report, we drag in the Political Department, the Revolutionary Tribunal, the remount officer.

I go to Jasiniewicze to exchange a carriage for a tachanka and horses. Incredibly dusty, hot. We go through Peresonnitsa. I feel lighthearted out in the fields, my 27th year. Thinking, the rye and barley are ripe, the oats look very good in places, the poppies are fading, no cherries left, the apples aren't ripe, a lot of flax, buckwheat, a lot of fields trampled down, hops.

Rich, but not unduly rich, land.

Dyakov, the remount officer—pantomime picture, red trousers with silver stripes, gold-embossed belt, from Stavropol, built like an Apollo, short gray moustache, 45, has a son and a nephew, fantastic oaths, they brought things from the supply department, he smashed a desk, but got what he wanted. Dyakov, the soldiers love him, our commander's a hero, was an athlete, barely literate, now "I'm Inspector of Cavalry," a general. Dyakov is a communist, brave, an old Budyonny man. Met a millionaire, with a lady on his arm— "tell me, Mr. Dyakov, haven't we met at the club?" "I've been in eight countries, when I take the stage I need only wink."

He's a dancer, concertina player, crafty, a tall-talker, most picturesque character. Has difficulty reading documents, keeps losing them, it's got me down, he says, all this paperwork, if I give up where will they be without me, his swearing, the way he talks to the peasants, they listen openmouthed.

A tachanka and a couple of skinny horses, about horses.

To Dyakov with my requests—phew, you'll drive me crazy, issuing linen, it's one thing after another, fatherly attitude, says (to a sick man): you'll be head drover here. I go home. Night. Staff work.

We're living in the house of the headman's mother. Our cheerful landlady speaks in a rapid gabble, tucks up her skirts and works like an ant, for her own family and an extra seven people. Cherkashin, Lepin's dispatch rider, insolent and pushy, gives them no peace, we're always asking for something, children wandering all over the place, we help ourselves to hay, the cottage is full of flies, children, and old people, the daughter-in-law, soldiers jostling and yelling. The old woman is sick. Old people come visiting, sit in mournful silence, a lamp.

Night, HQ, the high-falutin' telephonist, K. Karlych writing reports, dispatch riders and duty clerks sleeping, pitch dark in the village, a sleepy clerk types out an order, K. Karlych's clockwork precision, dispatch riders arrive silently.

The advance on Lutsk. Led by the 2nd Brigade, they haven't taken it yet. Where are our advance units?

Belyov. 14 July 1920

Sokolov is living with us. He's lying on hay, lanky, Russian-looking, in leather jackboots. Misha, a harmless, red-faced lad from Oryol. Lepin flirts with the hired girl when nobody's looking, his flat, tense face, our landlady gabbles away, her quaint sayings, works tirelessly, her old mother-in-law, a withered little old woman, loves her, Cherkashin, Lepin's dispatch rider, eggs her on, she rattles away without pause.

Lepin fell asleep at HQ, a completely idiotic look on his face, just couldn't wake up. Moaning in the village, the soldiers are changing horses, giving the peasants broken-down old nags in exchange, trampling the crops, driving off cattle, complaints to the chief of staff, Cherkashin is arrested for whipping a peasant. Lepin spends three hours writing a letter to the Tribunal, Cherkashin, he says, was influenced by the outrageously provocative remarks of Red Army officer Sokolov. I can only advise against putting seven soldiers in one cottage.

Gaunt, bad-tempered Sokolov tells me "we're destroying everything, I hate war."

What are they all doing here in this war, Zholnarkevich, Sokolov? It's all unconscious, inertial, unthinking. Some system.

Frank Mosher. American airman, shot down, barefoot but elegant, neck like a pillar, dazzlingly white teeth, clothes covered with oil and dirt. Asks me anxiously whether he's committed a crime, fighting against Soviet Russia. Our cause is strong. Ah, but all at once—the smell of Europe, its cafés, civilization, power, ancient culture, so many thoughts, I watch him, can't take my eyes off him. Letter from Major Fauntleroy—things bad in Poland, no constitution, Bolsheviks strong, socialists the center of attention but not in power. We must study the new methods of warfare. What are they telling Western European soldiers? Russian imperialism, they want to abolish nationhood, customs, that's the main thing—annex all the Slav lands, such antiquated words. Endless conversation with Mosher, I'm absorbed in old memories, they'll shake you up, Mosher, ah, Conan Doyle, letters to New York. Whether he's just putting on an act or not, Mosher is frantically eager to find out what Bolshevism is all about. Sad and delicious impression.

I'm getting used to HQ, I have a coachman, 39-year-old Grishchuk, prisoner of war in Germany for 6 years, 50 versts from home (he's from the Kremenets district), they won't give him leave, he says nothing.

Divisional Commander Timoshenko at HQ. A colorful figure. A colossus in red half-leather trousers, red cap, well-built, former platoon commander, was at one time a machine gunner, an artillery ensign. Fabulous stories. The commissar of the 1st Brigade was afraid of fire, the lads mounted, he starts using his whip on the regimental commanders, including Kniga, he shoots at the commissar, to horse you bastards, charges at them, 5 shots, comrades, help, I'll show you, shoots himself through the hand, through one eye, the revolver jams, I gave the commissar a dressing-down, he electrifies the Cossacks, a Budyonny man—go up forward with him and if the Poles don't kill you, he will.

The 2nd Brigade attacks Lutsk, withdraws early evening, enemy counterattack, in great force, trying to break through to Dubno. We have occupied Dubno.

Report—Minsk, Bobruisk, Molodechno, Proskurov, Sventsiany, Sarny, Staro-Konstantinov all taken, they're approaching Galicia, where a cavalry maneuver will be executed on the Styr or on the Bug. Kovel is being evacuated, large troop concentrations in Lvov, Mosher's testimony. An assault on the way.

The divisional commander's gratitude for the battle at Rovno. Transmit the order.

The village, deserted, a light at HQ, Jewish detainees. Budyonny's men bring communism, a woman weeps. Oh, what a dismal life Russians lead. What's become of Ukrainian gaiety? The harvest is beginning. Poppies are ripening, where can I get corn for the horses and cherry dumplings?

Which divisions are to the left of us?

Mosher barefoot, noon, stupid Lepin.

Belyov. 15 July 1920

Interrogating deserters. They show us some of our own leaflets. They are very effective, these leaflets help the Cossacks.

We have an interesting commissar—Bakhturov, a fighter, fat, swears a lot, always in the front line.

Describe the job of war correspondent, what is a war correspondent?

Have to get operational reports from Lepin, it's torment. HQ is set up in the house of a baptized Jew.

Dispatch riders stand outside the HQ building at night.

They've started mowing. I'm learning to recognize plants. My sister's birthday tomorrow.

Description of Volhynia. Revolting way the peasants live, dirty, we eat, lyrical Matyash, skirt-chaser, drawls more affectedly than ever even when talking to an old woman.

Lepin flirting with the hired girl.

Our units a verst and a half from Lutsk. The army is preparing for a cavalry attack, concentrating its forces in Lvov, moving them up toward Lutsk.

We've captured a proclamation by Piłsudski—"Warriors of the Rzecz Pospolita." A moving proclamation. "Our graves are white with the bones of five generations of warriors, our ideals, our Poland, our shining home, the eyes of your homeland are on you, it trembles, our young freedom, one more effort, our thoughts are of you, all for you, soldiers of the Rzecz Pospolita."

Touching, sad, no iron Bolshevik arguments, no promises, and words like *order, ideals, live in freedom.* Our side is winning!

Novoselki. 16 July 1920

Order from Army HQ received—seize the fords over the River Styr in the Rożyszcze-Jałowicze sector.

HQ moves to Novoselki, twenty-five versts away. I ride with the divisional commander, HQ Squadron, galloping horses, forest, oak trees, forest paths, the divisional commander's red cap, his powerful frame, buglers, beauty, a new army, the divisional commander and squadron a single body.

Our billet, young householders, quite well-off, there are pigs, a cow, and all they can say is "got none."

Zholnarkevich's story of the crafty medical orderly. Two women, had to find a way of dealing with them. Gave one castor oil, when it gripped her he got going on the other.

Terrible business, soldiers' love, two lusty Cossacks made a deal with the same woman. Can you take it, I can take it, one of them had three goes, the other moves in, she spins around the room, makes a mess all over the floor, they throw her out, don't pay her, she'd tried too hard.

On Budyonny's commanders—condottieri or future usurpers? They sprang from the Cossack milieu, that's the main thing—describe the origins of these units, all these Timoshenkos, the Budyonnys themselves handpicked the units—for the most part neighbors from their own village, now the units have been properly organized by the Soviet regime.

The division is carrying out its orders, a strong column is moving on Dubno from Lutsk, the order to evacuate Lutsk has obviously been cancelled, troops and equipment are arriving there.

With our young hosts. She is tall, with traces of rustic beauty, rummages around among 5 children sprawled out on the bench. Curious—each child looks after one of the others, "Mama, give him your titties." The mother, shapely and red-faced, lies with dignity in that heaving heap of children. The husband is a good sort. Sokolov: these whelps should be shot, why keep breeding them? Husband: they're little now, but they'll get bigger.

Describe our soldiers: Cherkashin (got back from the tribunal today looking a bit humbled)—insolent, gangling, depraved, what sort of citizen of communist Russia will he make, Matyash, the Ukrainian, infinitely lazy, a womanizer, always limp and listless, with his shoelaces untied, indolent movements, Sokolov's dispatch rider Misha, has been in Italy, handsome, slovenly.

Describe—riding with the divisional commander, a small squadron, the divisional commander's entourage, Bakhturov, the old Budyonny man, a march plays as we move out.

The divisional chief of staff sitting on a bench, a peasant choking with indignation, showing him the half-dead hack they've given him in exchange for a good horse. Dyakov arrives, the conversation is short, you can get 15 thousand for a horse like that, no, for a horse like that—20 thousand. If it gets to its feet—all right, it's a horse.

They take pigs, poultry—the village moans. Describe our supply system. I sleep in the cottage. The horror of their way of life. Flies.

Research on flies, myriads of them. Five unhappy little children, bawling.

They hide their foodstuffs from us.

Novoselki. 17 July 1920

I'm beginning my military journal from 16 July. I go to Pelcha—the Political Department, they're eating cucumbers, the sun's shining, men sleeping barefoot behind haystacks. Yakovlev promises his cooperation. The day passes in work. Lepin has a swollen lip. He stoops. Difficult to get on with. A new page—I'm studying the science of military operations.

By one of the cottages—a cow, recently calved, with its throat cut. Bluish teats on the ground, just skin. Indescribable pity! A murdered young mother.

Novoselki—Malyi Dorogostai. 18 July 1920

The Polish army is concentrating in the Dubno-Kremenets region for the decisive offensive. We are paralyzing their maneuvers and will forestall them. The army is going over to the offensive in the southern sector, our division is in reserve. Our orders are to seize the crossings over the Styr in the Lutsk region.

We're moving out in the morning toward Malyi Dorogostai (north of Młynów), leaving the wagon train behind, also the sick and the administrative staff, there's obviously an engagement ahead of us.

An order comes from the Southwest Army Group: when we enter Galicia—the first time Soviet troops cross the frontier—we are to treat the population well. We are not entering a conquered country, the country belongs to the workers and peasants of Galicia, and to them alone, we are going there to help them establish Soviet rule. An important and sensible order, but will the scavengers obey it? No.

We move out. Buglers. The divisional commander's dazzling service cap. Talk with the div. commander about how I need a horse.

We ride on, forests, harvesters, not many though, it's poor, a couple of women and old men here and there. The centuries-old Volhynian forests—majestic green oaks and hornbeams, you can see why the oak is tsar.

We ride along narrow paths with two HQ squadrons, they always accompany the div. commander, they're crack troops. Describe the trappings of their horses, the sabers sheathed in scarlet velvet, curved sabers, their waistcoats, the rugs on their saddles. They are poorly dressed, though every one of them has ten service jackets, it's the fashion, no doubt.

Plowed fields, roads, sun, ripening wheat, we trample the fields, the harvest is poor, stunted grain crops, many Czech, Polish, and German settlements hereabouts. Different people, signs of prosperity, cleanliness, magnificent orchards, we eat unripe apples and pears, everyone wants to be billeted on the foreigners, I catch myself wanting it, the foreigners are scared.

The Jewish cemetery outside Malin, hundreds of years old, gravestones have toppled over, almost all the same shape, oval at the top, the cemetery is overgrown with grass, it has seen Khmelnitsky, now Budyonny, unfortunate Jewish population, everything repeats itself, now that whole story—Poles, Cossacks, Jews—is repeating itself with stunning exactitude, the only new element is communism.

More and more frequently we come across trenches from the last war, there's barbed wire everywhere, enough for fences for the next ten years or so, ruined villages, people everywhere trying to rebuild, but not very successfully, they have nothing, no building materials, no cement.

With the Cossacks when they stop for a rest, hay for the horses, every one of them has a long story to tell—Denikin, farmsteads of their own, their own leaders, the Budyonnys and the Knigas, campaigns with 200 men, bandit raids, the rich, free Cossack life, how many officers' heads they've cut off. They read the newspaper, but the names don't sink in, it's so easy to get everything turned around.

Splendid comradeship, solidarity, love of horses, a Cossack's horse occupies a quarter of his day, endless bartering, arguments. The role and life of the horse.

Their behavior toward their superiors is quite unique—simple, familiar.

Malyi Dorogostai was completely destroyed, is rebuilding. We ride into the priest's orchard. We help ourselves to hay, eat the fruit, a beautiful orchard, shady and sunny, a little white church, used to be cows, horses, a little priest with a pigtail goes around looking lost, collecting receipts. Bakhturov lies on his belly eating curds and cherries, says I'll give you receipts, honest I will.

We've gobbled enough for a year at the priest's place. He's as good as ruined, they say he's looking for a job—"do you have regimental chaplains?"

Evening in the billet. "Got none" again, they all lie, I write my journal, they give me potatoes and butter. Night in the village, an enormous circle of crimson fire before my eyes, yellow fields flee from the ruined village. Night. Lights at HQ. There are always lights at HQ, Karl Karlovich is dictating an order from memory, he never forgets anything, the telephonists sit there with drooping heads. Karl Karlovich once served in Warsaw.

Malyi Dorogostai—Smordva—Berezhtsy. 19 July 1920

Slept badly last night. Shooting pains in my stomach. We ate green pears yesterday. I feel rotten. We move out at dawn.

The enemy is attacking in the Młynów-Dubno sector. We have forced our way into Radziwiłłów.

The decisive attack by all divisions—from Lutsk to Kremenets— began today at dawn. The 5th and 6th Divisions are concentrated in Smordva, we have reached Kozino.

Which means we are bearing south.

We move out of Malyi Dorogostai. The div. commander greets his squadrons, his horse trembles. The band plays. Our column is strung out along the road. The road is unbearable. We go by way of Młynów toward Berezhtsy, we cannot enter Młynów (a Jewish town). We approach Berezhtsy. Its guns open up, our headquarters staff turn back, there is a smell of fuel oil, cavalry units creep along the slopes. Smordva, the priest's house, provincial ladies with tear-stained faces and white stockings, I've seen nothing like them for ages, the priest's wife wounded, limps, the wiry priest, a stoutly built house, the chief of staff and commander of 14th Division, we wait for the brigades to move in, our HQ staff stands on high ground, a truly Bolshevik staff—Div. Commander Bakhturov with his commissars. We are under fire. The div. commander is a devil of a fellow, clever, energetic, a bit of a dandy, sure of himself, he thought up the encircling move against Bokunin, the attack is held up, orders to the brigades. Kolesov and Kniga (the famous Kniga, why is he famous) galloped in. Kolesov's magnificent horse, Kniga has a face like a counterhand in a bakery, a businesslike Ukrainian. Orders issued quickly, all consult each other, the bombardment gets heavier, shells fall a hundred yards away.

The commander of 14th Division is made of poorer stuff, stupid, garrulous, an intellectual, likes to pretend he's a Budyonny man, swears incessantly, "I've been fighting all night," likes to boast a bit. The brigades are winding their way along the opposite bank in long ribbons, the supply wagons are under fire, pillars of dust. Budyonny's regiments with their wagon trains, rugs over their saddles.

I feel worse and worse. My temperature is 39.8. Budyonny and Voroshilov arrive.

Conference. The div. commander flies past. The battle begins. I lie in the priest's garden. Grishchuk is completely apathetic. What Grishchuk is like: submissive, eternally quiet, infinitely sluggish. He's fifty versts from home, hasn't been there in six years, and doesn't run away.

He knows what obeying your superiors means, the Germans taught him.

The wounded start coming in, bandages, bare bellies, long-suffering, unbearable heat, shot at from both sides, no letup, impossible to doze off. Budyonny and Voroshilov on the porch. Battle picture, the cavalry return, dust-stained, sweating, red-faced, no trace of excitement after their butcher's work, professionals, it's all done perfectly calmly—that's what makes them special, their self-assurance, hard work, nurses on horseback gallop by, an armored car. Opposite us Count Ledochowski's mansion, a white building overlooking a lake, not very high, not ostentatious, the essence of nobility, I remember my childhood, novels—and much else. At the medical assistant's—a pathetic, good-looking young Jew, perhaps he was on the count's payroll, gray in the face with worry. Excuse me, what is the situation at the front? The Poles mocked and tormented him, he thinks that life will begin now, Cossacks, however, don't always behave well.

Echoes of battle—galloping horsemen, situation reports, the wounded, the killed.

I sleep by the churchyard wall. Some brigade commander is asleep there with his head on the belly of some young lady.

I broke into a sweat, and it helped. I ride to Berezhtsy, the office staff are there, a ruined house, I drink cherry tea, lie down in the landlady's bed, sweat, take aspirin powder. If only I could sleep. I remember—I have a fever, it is sultry, soldiers making a noise in the churchyard, others cool and collected, they let the stallions in.

Berezhtsy, Sienkiewicz, I drink cherry tea, lie down on a spring mattress, some child is breathing with difficulty nearby. Lost consciousness for a couple of hours. Somebody wakes me up. I'm drenched in sweat. We ride back to Smordva in the night, ride on farther, keeping to the edge of the forest. Riding at night, moon, squadron somewhere ahead.

Cottage in the forest. Peasants and their wives sleeping along the walls. Konstantin Karlovich dictating. A rare sight—the squadron sleeping round about, everything dark, nothing can be seen, cold air from the forest, I bump into horses, at HQ people eating, I feel ill, I lie down on the ground near a tachanka, sleep 3 hours covered with Barsukov's shawl and greatcoat, comfortable.

Isaac Babel in 1920 (courtesy A. N. Pirozhkova)

Red Cavalrymen near Maikop in the Northern Caucasus, shortly before the Polish campaign, 1920 (reprinted from S. M. Budyonny, *The Path of Valour* [Moscow: Progress, 1972])

General Semyon Mikhailovich Budyonny (second from right) and Commissar Kliment Efremovich Voroshilov (far right) with officers of the First Cavalry Army's Fourteenth Division, 1920 (reprinted from S. M. Budyonny, *Proidennyi put'* [Moscow: Defense Ministry Publishing House, 1973], vol. 3)

Tachankas of a First Cavalry Army Brigade, 1920
(reprinted from Budyonny, *Proidennyi put'*)

(*left*) Semyon Konstantinovich Timoshenko, commander of the Sixth Division
until early August (and prototype of Babel's "Savitsky") (*right*) Iosif Rodionovich
Apanasenko, commander of the Sixth Division from early August to October (and
prototype of Babel's "Pavlichenko") (reprinted from Budyonny, *The Path of Valour*)

Refugees in the Volhynian countryside, 1920
(courtesy Pilsudski Institute Archives)

Eastern Poland, 1920 (courtesy Pilsudski Institute Archives)

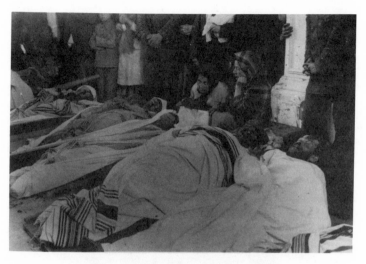

Casualties of the June 1920 pogrom in Zhitomir
(courtesy YIVO Institute for Jewish Research)

Jewish street in Rovno on a Sunday, 1920–30 (photo Alter Kacyzne;
courtesy YIVO Institute for Jewish Research)

A synagogue in Dubno (courtesy YIVO Institute
for Jewish Research)

Alexander Street in Dubno, undated, pre–World War II (reprinted from *Dubno: A Memorial to the Jewish Community of Dubno, Wolyn* [in Hebrew and Yiddish], ed. Ya'acov Adini [Tel Aviv: Dubno Organization in Israel, 1966])

The Market in Berestechko, undated, pre–World War II (reprinted from *There Was a Town . . . Memorial Book of Berestechko and Vicinity* [in Hebrew and Yiddish]), ed. M. Singer [Haifa: Association of Former Residents of Berestechko in Israel, 1961])

A Polish manor of the eastern borderlands, 1920
(courtesy Pilsudski Institute Archives)

20 July 1920. The Smordva Heights. Pelcha

We move out at 5 a.m. Rain, damp, we keep to the woods. The operation is going well, our divisional commander has chosen the right way round, we continue our circular movement. We're soaked through, forest paths. The encircling movement takes us by way of Bokuika toward Pelcha. Information received, Dobryvodka taken at 10 a.m., Kozin at 12 after minimum resistance. We are pursuing the enemy, advancing on Pelcha. Forests, forest paths, the squadrons snaking along ahead of us.

My health is improving, for some inexplicable reason.

I am studying the flora of Volhynia, much felling, forest thinned around the edges, relics of the war, barbed wire, white trenches. Majestic green oaks, hornbeams, many pines, willows—a majestic yet friendly tree the willow—rain in the forest, washed-out roads, ash trees.

By forest paths to Pelcha. We arrive about 10 o'clock. Yet another village, a lanky landlady, that tiresome "got none," very clean, son was in the army, gives us eggs, no milk, unbearably stuffy in the cottage, rain, washes out all the roads, black, squelchy mud, can't get through to HQ. I sit in the cottage all day, it's warm, raining outside. I find this life so flat, so boring—the chickens, the hidden cow, the mud, the stupidity. An inexpressible misery brooding over the earth, everything damp, black, autumn, while back home in Odessa . . .

In Pelcha we seized the wagon train of the 49th Polish Infantry Regiment. The share-out takes place under my window, with a lot of completely idiotic swearing, no end to it, some of the words are boring, I couldn't be bothered repeating them, about swearing, God's mother, sod's mother, the peasant women cringe, children ask about it—the soldiers go on swearing. God's mother, sod's mother. I'll shoot, hit him.

I get a bag for documents and a saddlebag. Describe this muddled life. The Polish peasant can't go to work in his field. I sleep on the landlady's bed. We've heard that England put forward a plan for peace between Soviet Russia and Poland. Could it possibly be over soon?

21 July 1920. Pelcha—Boratyn

We have taken Dubno. The resistance, whatever we say, was minimal. Why? Prisoners tell us, and we can see for ourselves—a revolution of the little people. There's a lot you could say about it, the beauty of the Polish facade, there is something touching about it all, my countess. Fate, Polish honor, the Jews, Count Ledochowski. Proletarian revolution. How eagerly I breathe in the secent of Europe—blowing from out there.

We leave for Boratyn by way of Dobryvodka, forests, fields, gentle contours, oaks, yet again the band playing and the div. commander, and somewhere on the sidelines—a war. A stop for rest in Zabokriki, I eat white bread. Grishchuk horrifies me sometimes—has he been knocked silly? The Germans, that tirelessly chewing jaw.

Describe Grishchuk.

In Boratyn—a sturdy, sunny village. Chmil laughing at his daughter, a taciturn but rich peasant, eggs fried in butter, milk, white bread, gluttony, sunshine, cleanliness, I am getting over my illness, all the peasants look alike to me, a young mother. Grishchuk is radiant, they gave him an omelette with fatback, a beautiful, shady threshing barn, clover. Why doesn't Grishchuk desert?

A beautiful day. My interview with Konstantin Karlovich. What sort of person is our Cossack? Many-layered: looting, reckless daring, professionalism, revolutionary spirit, bestial cruelty. We are the vanguard, but of what? The population await their saviors, the Jews look for liberation—and in ride the Kuban Cossacks . . .

The army commander summons the divisional commander to Kozin for consultation. 7 versts away. I go with him. Sands. Every house remains in my heart. Clusters of Jews. Their faces—this is the ghetto, and we are an ancient people, exhausted, but we still have some strength left, a shop, I drink splendid coffee, I pour balm on the soul of the shopkeeper, who is listening to the noise in his shop.

Cossacks yelling, swearing, climbing over the shelves, too bad for the shop, sweating, ginger-bearded Jew. I wander around endlessly, can't tear myself away, the town was destroyed, is rebuilding, has existed four hundred years, remains of a synagogue, magnificent old temple in ruins, what was a Catholic and is now an Orthodox church, enchantingly white, with triple door, visible from afar, now Orthodox. An old Jew—I like talking with my own kind— they understand me. Cemetery, Rabbi Azrael's ruined house, three generations, the gravestone under a tree that has grown up over it, those old stones, all the same shape, with the same message, this exhausted Jew who is my guide, a family of stupid-looking, thick-legged Jews living in a wooden shed by the cemetery, graves of three Jewish soldiers, killed in the Russo-German war. The Abramoviches from Odessa, the mother came for the burial, and I can see this Jewish woman, burying a son killed in battle for a cause which to her is revolting, incomprehensible, criminal.

An old and a new cemetery—the town is four hundred years old.

Evening, I walk around among the houses, Jewish men and women reading posters and proclamations, "Poland is the running dog of the bourgeoisie" and so on. "Insects can kill" and "do not remove stoves from heated boxcars."

These Jews are like portraits, elongated, silent, long-bearded, not like our type, fat and jovial. Lofty old men, hanging around with nothing to do. Most important—the shop and the cemetery.

Back seven versts to Boratyn, beautiful evening, my heart is full, rich householders, pert girls, fried eggs, fatback, our soldiers catching flies, the Russo-Ukrainian soul. I'm not sure I'm really interested.

22 July 1920. Boratyn

Before lunch—a report to army field HQ. Fine sunny weather, rich, thriving village, I go to the mill, what a watermill is like, the Jewish millhand, afterward I bathe in a cold, shallow stream under the not very hot sun of Volhynia. Two little girls playing in the water, I feel a strange desire, suppressed with difficulty, to use foul language, crude obscenities.

Sokolov is unwell. I provide horses to send him to the hospital. HQ staff are leaving for Leszniów (Galicia—the first time we cross the frontier). I'm waiting for horses. It's nice in the village, plenty of light, food.

Two hours later I set off for Khotin. The road runs through the forest, I feel uneasy. Grishchuk stupid, alarming. I'm on Sokolov's heavy horse. I'm the only one on the road. It's very light, the air is clear, not too hot, just pleasantly warm. A cart up ahead, five men, look like Poles. A game, we ride along, pull up, where are you coming from? Mutual alarm and fear. We see our own troops outside Khotin, we ride in, shots fired. Gallop wildly back, I tug my horse along with the rein. Bullets hum past, whistle. Artillery fire. Grishchuk sometimes rushes around with a morose and silent energy, then at moments of danger gets obtuse, lifeless, dark, there's heavy growth on his jaw. Nobody left in Boratyn. Supply wagons outside Boratyn, beginning of a hopeless muddle. The epic of the wagon train, revulsion and nastiness. Gusev in command. We spend half the night outside Kozin, exchanging fire. We send out scouts, nobody knows anything, men riding around all over the place looking efficient, a tall German—the district commandant, night, feeling sleepy, helpless, you don't know where you're being taken, I think it's 20 or 30 of those we drove into the forest attacking us. But where did the artillery come from? I fall asleep for half an hour, they tell me there's been an exchange of shots, our side have sent a cordon out. We move on. The horses are exhausted, a horrible night, this enormous wagon train of ours moving through pitch darkness, nobody knows through which villages, there's a big fire off to one side, other wagons cross our track—is the front crumbling, or is it just a baggage train panic?

The night drags on endlessly, we land in a ditch, Grishchuk has a strange way of driving, somebody's shaft rams us from behind, shouting some distance away, we halt every half verst and stand there aimlessly, for an excruciatingly long time.

One rein snaps, the tachanka won't respond, we ride off the road into a field, into the night, Grishchuk has a fit of stupid, hopeless, animal despair which infuriates me: Oh, let the reins go up in flames, oh, burn away, burn away. He is blind—he admits it, Grishchuk does, he can't see a thing at night. The wagon train is leaving us behind, the roads are difficult, black mud, Grishchuk, clutching the remnant of the broken rein, says in his surprisingly sonorous tenor—we're done for, the Pole will catch up with us, there's gunfire all around, we wagoners are caught in a ring. We drive on with our broken rein, following our noses, the tachanka creaks pitifully, there's a miserable dull dawn in the distance, wet fields. Violet streaks in the sky, black hollows in between. At dawn—the village of Verba. A railbed, dead, shallow, the smell of Galicia. 4 o'clock in the morning.

23 July 1920. In Verba

The Jews, after a sleepless night, stand around pathetically, birdlike, blue in the face, disheveled, in waistcoats and without socks. A wet, cheerless dawn, Verba is choked with supply wagons, thousands of carts, all the drivers have the same features, first-aid units, staff of the 45th Division, depressing, probably nonsensical rumors, despite our string of victories . . . Two brigades of the 11th Division taken prisoner, the Poles have seized Kozin, unhappy Kozin, what will happen there. The strategic situation is peculiar. The 6th Division is in Leszniów, the Poles are in Kozin, in Boratyn, in our rear, we're like squashed pies. We wait on the road out of Verba. We stand there two hours. Misha, wearing a tall white hat with a red ribbon, gallops across the field. Everyone eats—bread with straw in it, green apples, dirty revolting food put into foul mouths by dirty fingers. We ride on. It's astonishing—tie-ups every five paces, endless lines of supply wagons belonging to the 45th and 11th Divisions, we keep losing our own baggage train and finding it again. Fields with trampled wheat, or cropped bare by horses, villages not quite eaten bare, hilly terrain, where shall we end up? The road to

Dubno. The forest, magnificent, shady, ancient forest. Fierce heat, shade in the forest. Many trees felled for military needs—damn them—bare patches bristling with stumps at the forest's edges. The ancient Volhynian forests of Dubno, must find out where to get honey, dark, fragrant honey.

Describe the forest.

Krivikha, ruined Czechs, a toothsome woman. What follows is horrible. She cooks for 100 people, flies, the commissar's Shurka, sweaty and all shaken-up, fresh meat with potatoes, they take all the hay, reap the oats, potatoes by the pood, the servant girl is run off her feet, remnants of a well-run farm. Pitiful lanky, smiling Czech, plump, pretty, foreign woman, his wife.

A bacchanal. Gusev's toothsome Shurka with his retinue, Red Army men—the riffraff, wagoners, the whole mob tramping round the kitchen, helping themselves to potatoes, ham, they're baking flatcakes. The heat is unbearable, stifling, clouds of flies. Czechs at the end of their tether. Loud voices, coarse behavior, greed. Still, I get a splendid dinner, roast pork with potatoes, and splendid coffee. After dinner I sleep under the trees—a gentle, shady slope, a swing flying back and forth before my eyes. Before my eyes— gentle green and yellow hills, flooded with sunshine, and forests, the Dubno forests. I sleep three hours. Then to Dubno. I ride with Prishchepa, a new acquaintance, caftan, white hood, an illiterate communist, he takes me to see his Zhenya. The husband—a grober mensch—rides around the villages on a wretched nag buying up produce from the peasants. The wife is buxom, languid, roguish, a sensual young Jewess, married 5 months, doesn't like her husband, but that's all nonsense, she's playing with Prishchepa. I am the center of attention, "er ist ein [illegible]," she keeps glancing at me, asks my surname, can't keep her eyes off me, we drink tea, I'm in an idiotic position, I stay quiet, limp, polite, say thank you for every move she makes. Before my eyes—the life of a Jewish family, the mother arrives, some young ladies, Prishchepa is quite the ladies' man. Dubno has changed hands several times. Our troops apparently didn't sack the place. Now everybody's trembling again, and again the endless self-abasement, and hatred of the

Poles, who pluck their beards. The husband—will there be freedom to trade, to buy a bit of something and sell it straight off, not to profiteer. I say there will be, everything's changing for the better—my usual system—miraculous things are happening in Russia—express trains, free food for children, theaters, the International. They listen with delight and disbelief. I think—you'll have your diamond-studded sky, everything and everyone will be turned upside down and inside out for the umpteenth time, and feel sorry for them.

Dubno synagogues. Everything destroyed. Two little vestibules left, centuries, two tiny rooms, everything full of memories, four synagogues, close together, then pasture, plowed fields, the setting sun. The synagogues are ancient buildings, squat, green and blue, the Hasidic synagogue, inside, nondescript architecture. I go into the Hasidic synagogue. It's Friday. Such misshapen little figures, such worn faces, it all came alive for me, what it was like three hundred years ago, the old men running about the synagogue, no wailing, for some reason they keep moving from corner to corner, their worship could not be less formal. Of all the Jews in Dubno the most repulsive looking seem to have gathered here. I pray, or rather almost pray, thinking of Hershele and how to describe him. A quiet evening in the synagogue, that always has an irresistible effect on me, four synagogues in a row. Religion? There are no adornments in the building, everything is white and plain to the point of asceticism, everything is fleshless, bloodless, to a grotesque degree, you have to have the soul of a Jew to sense what it means. But what does the soul consist of? Can it be that ours is the century in which they perish?

A corner of Dubno, four synagogues, Friday evening, Jewish men and women by the ruined stones—all fixed in memory. Then evening, herring, I'm sad because I've no one to go to bed with. Prishchepa and the tantalizing, irritating Zhenya, her eyes Jewish and sparkling, her fat legs and soft bosom. Prishchepa, his hands sinking deeper and deeper, her insistent gaze, her fool of a husband feeding his exchanged horse in the tiny byre.

We spend the night with some other Jews, Prishchepa asks them to play him something, the fat boy with the solid, dull-witted face, breathless with terror, says that he's not in the mood. The horse is in a little yard opposite. Grishchuk is fifty versts from home. Doesn't run away.

The Poles are attacking in the Kozin-Boratyn region, they are in our rear, 6th Division is in Leszniów, Galicia. The operation is aimed at Brody, with Radziwiłłów ahead and one brigade to the rear. 6th Division is involved in heavy fighting.

24 July 1920

Morning—at army HQ. 6th Division is mopping up the enemy attacking us in Khotin, the battle zone is between Khotin and Kozin, and I think, unlucky Kozin.

Cemetery, rounded gravestones.

Ride with Prishchepa from Krivikha to Leszniów via Demidovka. Prishchepa's soul—an illiterate boy, a communist, parents killed by Kadets, tells how he went round the village collecting his property. A picturesque figure with his hood, as simple as a blade of grass, will be a looter, despises Grishchuk because he doesn't like or understand horses. Our route is through Khorupan, Smordva, and Demidovka. Must memorize the picture—wagons, riders, half-ruined villages, fields and woods, oaks, now and then wounded men and my tachanka.

In Demidovka by evening. A Jewish town, I'm on my guard. Jews scattered about on the outskirts, everything has been destroyed. We are in a house with a mob of women. The Lachecki family, the Szwechwels—no, this isn't Odessa. A dentist—Dora Aronovna, reads Artsybashev, with Cossacks on the loose all around. She is haughty, angry, says that the Poles have forfeited their self-respect, despises the communists for their plebeian ways, a horde of daughters in white stockings, pious father and mother. Every daughter a distinct personality—one pathetic, black-haired, bandy-legged, another—an opulent beauty, a third—housewifely, and all of them, probably, old maids.

Main cause of discord—today is the Sabbath. Prishchepa tries to make them fry potatoes but tomorrow is a fast day, the 9th of Av, and I keep quiet, because I'm a Russian. The dentist, pale with pride and a sense of her own dignity, declares that no one is going to dig potatoes because it is a holiday.

Prishchepa, restrained by me for quite a while, finally breaks out—fucking Yids, the whole arsenal of abuse, they all, hating us and me, go and dig potatoes, afraid in someone else's garden, they blame crosses, Prishchepa seethes. How excrutiating it all is—Artsybashev, the orphaned schoolgirl from Rovno, Prishchepa in his hood. The mother wrings her hands—a fire lit on the Sabbath, bad language flying around. Budyonny has been here and left. Argument between a Jewish youth and Prishchepa. The youth wears glasses, is dark-haired, nervous, has scarlet inflamed eyelids, speaks Russian incorrectly. He believes in God, says God is an ideal we carry in our souls, every person has in his soul his own God, if you behave badly God grieves—this foolishness is pronounced in an exalted fashion and as if it hurt. Prishchepa is insultingly stupid, he goes on about religion in antiquity, confuses Christianity and paganism, his main point is that in antiquity there were communes, of course, he babbles incoherently, says your education is nonexistent, and the Jew has gone through sixth form at the Rovno gymnasium—he parrots Platonov, it's touching and comic—clans, clan elders, Perun, paganism.

We eat like oxen, fried potatoes and five tumblersful of coffee each. We sweat, they keep serving us, all this is terrible, I tell them fairy tales about Bolshevism—the blossoming, the express trains, Moscow's textile mills, universities, free meals, the Revel delegation, to crown it all the story of the Chinese, and I captivate all these tormented people. It's the 9th of Av. The old woman sobs, sitting on the floor, and her son, who worships his mother and says he believes in God just to please her, sings in a pleasant, light tenor, and tells the story of the destruction of the Temple. The terrible words of the prophet—they eat dung, their maidens are ravished, their menfolk killed, Israel subjugated, words of wrath and sorrow. The lamp smokes, the old woman wails, the young man sings melodiously, girls in white stockings, outside—Demidovka, night, Cossacks, all just as it was when the Temple was destroyed. I go out to sleep in the yard, stinking and damp.

Trouble with Grishchuk—he's in some sort of trance, goes around like a sleepwalker, doesn't feed the horses properly, reports problems too late, panders to the muzhiks and their children.

Machine gunners have ridden in from their posts, they stay over in our yard, it's night, they're wearing felt cloaks. Prishchepa is making up to a Jewish woman from Kremenets, good-looking, plump, in a sleek dress. She blushes prettily, her father-in-law, blind in one eye, is sitting close by, she blossoms, Prishchepa is easy to talk to, she blossoms and behaves coquettishly, what can they be talking about, then—he wants to go to bed, to pass the time, she is in agonies, who understands her soul better than I? He says—we'll write to each other, I think with anguish, surely she's not going to, Prishchepa talks on—she's agreeable (with him they're all agreeable). I remember that he probably has syphilis, it's doubtful whether he was ever fully cured.

The girl later on—I'll scream. Describe their initial delicate conversations, and what are you thinking about—she's a cultured person, has worked in the Revolutionary Committee.

My God, I think, women nowadays hear all that foul language, live like soldiers, what's become of gentler feelings?

In the night storm and rain, we run for the stable, it's dirty, dark, damp, cold, the machine gunners are packed off to their posts at dawn, they assemble in the pouring rain, felt cloaks and freezing rain. Pitiful Demidovka.

25 July 1920

We leave Demidovka in the morning. A painful two hours, the Jewish women were woken up at 4 a.m. and made to cook Russian meat, this on the 9th of Av. The girls run around the wet gardens half-naked and disheveled, importunate lust gets the better of Prishchepa, he falls on the girl engaged to the one-eyed old man's son, meanwhile they're commandeering the cart, an unbelievable swearing match is going on, other soldiers are eating meat from mess tins, she: I'll scream, her face, he pins her to the wall, an ugly scene. She does all she can to save the cart, they had hidden her in the attic, she'll be a good Jewish girl. She wrangles with the commissar, who says the Jews don't want to help the Red Army.

I lost my briefcase, then found it at HQ of the 14th Division in Lishnia.

We are making for Ostrów, 15 versts away, from there the road runs to Leszniów, it's dangerous there, Polish patrols. The priest, his daughter, looks like Plevitskaya or a jolly skeleton. She's a Kiev student, everyone is desperate for a little politeness, I tell my fairy tales, she can't tear herself away. 15 dangerous versts, sentries gallop up, we cross the border, wooden planks. Trenches everywhere.

We arrive at HQ Leszniów. A half-ruined town. The Russians have fouled the place up pretty thoroughly. A Catholic church, a Uniate church, a synagogue, beautiful buildings, a miserable life, some spectral Jews, revolting landlady, Galician, flies and filth, a lanky half-wild booby, Slavs Grade 2. Try to convey the spirit of ruined Leszniów, its enfeeblement, the dreary, half-foreign filth.

I sleep in the threshing barn. There is fighting around Brody and the crossing at Czurowice. Circulars about Soviet Galicia. Pastors. Night in Leszniów. How unimaginably sad it is, these Galicians grown wild and pitiful, and the ruined synagogues, and this petty life against a background of fearful events, of which only feeble reflections reach us.

26 July 1920. Leszniów

The Ukraine is in flames. Wrangel has not been liquidated. Makhno is making raids in Yekaterinoslav and Poltava provinces. New robber gangs have appeared, there is an uprising in the Kherson region. Why are they rebelling, doesn't the communist jacket fit?

What's happening to Odessa, homesick.

A lot of work, trying to reconstruct past events. Brody taken this morning, the enemy was surrounded yet again but got away, a sharp order from Budyonny—we've let them escape four times, we're good at shaking them up, but not tough enough to hold them.

Conference at Kozin, Budyonny's speech, no more maneuvering, only frontal attacks now, we keep losing contact with the enemy, no reconnaissance, no security, div. commanders show no initiative, there's no life in their operations.

I talk to some Jews—for the first time, not very interesting Jews. To one side a ruined synagogue, a red-haired man from Brody, townsmen of mine from Odessa.

I move in with a legless Jew, prosperity, cleanliness, quiet, splendid coffee, clean children, the father lost both legs on the Italian front, a new house, they're still building, the wife is mercenary, but decent, polite, a small, shady room, I find relief from the Galicians.

I feel anguished, I need to think about it all, Galicia, the world war, my own destiny.

The life of our division. About Bakhturov, about the div. commander, about the Cossacks, the looting, the avant-garde of the avant-garde. I am an outsider.

In the evening a panic, the enemy had pushed us out of Czurowice, and was a verst and a half from Leszniów. The div. commander galloped off and came galloping back. Our wanderings begin again, another sleepless night, wagon trains, the mysterious Grishchuk, the horses move noiselessly, men swearing, forests, stars, we halt somewhere or other. At dawn—Brody, the whole thing is horrible, barbed wire everywhere, burned-out chimneys, a town almost bled dry, dreary houses, they say there are some goods here, our men won't overlook them, there were factories here once, a Russian military cemetery, and—to judge by the lonely, nameless crosses on graves—these were indeed Russian soldiers.

A completely white road, felled trees, everything disfigured, Galicians on the roads, Austrian uniforms, barefoot men with pipes in their mouths, what's written on their faces, some secret of insignificance, banality, submissiveness.

Radziwiłłów—worse than Brody, barbed wire on posts, handsome buildings, daybreak, pitiful figures, fruit trees stripped, shabby Jews yawning, broken roadways, desecrated calvaries, a poorly endowed land, battered Catholic churches, where are the priests—but there were smugglers here once, and I can see life as it used to be.

Khotin. 27 July 1920

From Radziwiłłów—endless villages, horsemen galloping up forward, feel terrible after sleepless night.

Khotin is the same village in which we came under fire. My quarters are horrible—poverty, the bathhouse, flies, peasants, the man staid, mild, trim, the woman crafty, won't give us anything, I get hold of some fatback, potatoes. They live a ridiculous, solitary life, one little room and myriads of flies, horrible food, and they don't want anything better—miserliness, and the revolting, once-and-for-all way their dwelling is furnished, the hides stinking in the sun outside, the endless filth, all this exasperates me.

There was a local gentleman landowner, one Sveshnikov, his factory is a ruin, his manor house a ruin, the majestic skeleton of the factory, a redbrick building, tree-lined walks once, no trace now, the peasants don't care.

Supplies for our artillery are lagging. I'm getting the hang of staff work—the loathsome trade of murder. Communism's great merit—there's no preaching of hostility toward the enemy—except, it's true, toward Polish soldiers.

Prisoners were brought in, one, completely fit, was then shot and wounded twice by a Red Army man for no reason at all. The Pole writhed and groaned, they put a pillow under his head.

Zinoviev killed, a young communist in red trousers, the hoarse rattle in his throat, eyelids dark blue.

Astounding rumors—armistice talks begin on the 30th.

At night in a stinking hole calling itself a yard. Can't sleep, late, walk to HQ, the river crossing isn't going all that brilliantly.

Late night, red flag, silence, Red Army men hungry for women.

28 July 1920. Khotin

Battle for the crossing at Czurowice. 2nd Brigade, in Budyonny's presence, bleeds profusely. The whole infantry battalion wounded, nearly all killed. The Poles in old, screened trenches. Our side couldn't get a result. Is Polish resistance growing stronger?

No sign of disintegration in expectation of peace.

I am living in a poor cottage, where a son with a big head plays the violin. I terrorize the old woman, she doesn't give us anything. Grishchuk, turned to stone, neglects the horses, apparently schooled by hunger.

A ruined business, Sveshnikov, the landed gentleman, the majestic distillery in ruins (symbol of a Russian gentleman?), when they issued vodka all the troops drank themselves sick.

I am exasperated—can't get over my indignation, the filth, the apathy, the hopelessness of Russian life are unbearable, revolution will have some effect here.

The landlady conceals her pigs and her cow, talks rapidly, unctuously, and with impotent malice, she is idle and I feel that she is destroying their livelihood, her husband believes in authority, is charming, gentle, passive, resembles Stroyev.

It's boring in this village, life here is horrible. I immerse myself in staff work. Describe the day—reverberations of the battle in progress a few versts away, dispatch riders, Lepin has a swollen hand.

Red Army men are sleeping with the peasant women.

A story—a Polish regiment laid down their arms four times and each time had to defend themselves again when we began butchering them.

Evening, it's quiet, conversation with Matyazh, he is infinitely lazy, languid, a bit of a baby, and somehow inoffensively, affectionately lascivious. A terrible truth—all the soldiers have syphilis. Matyazh is getting better (with hardly any treatment). He had syphilis once, got cured in two weeks, he and a friend of his were supposed to pay ten silver kopecks in Stavropol, the friend died, Misha has had it several times, Senechka and Gerasya both have syphilis, they all go to the village women, although they have fiancées at home. The scourge of the soldiery, Russia's scourge. It's terrifying. They eat crushed crystal, drink either carbolic acid or a solution of ground glass. All our fighting men—velvet caps, rape, forelocks, battles, revolution and syphilis. All Galicia is infected.

Letter to Zhenya, missing her and home.

Must keep an eye on the Special Section and the Revolutionary Tribunal.

Will there really be peace talks on the 30th?

Order from Budyonny. We have let the enemy get away for the fourth time, he was completely surrounded at Brody.

Describe Matyazh, Misha. The peasants, I'd like to figure them out.

We have the forces to maneuver and surround the Poles, but our grip, basically, is weak, and they break out, Budyonny is angry, reprimands the div. commander. Write up biographies of the div. commander, Military Commissar Kniga, and others.

29 July 1920. Leszniów

In the morning we leave for Leszniów. With my former landlord again, black-bearded, legless Froim. During my absence he has been robbed of four thousand guldens and, for good measure, his boots. His wife is a fawning bitch, but colder to me, she can see she's not going to get rich out of me, how greedy they are. I speak to her in German. Bad weather is setting in.

Froim has lame children, lots of them, I can't tell one from another, he keeps his cow and his horse out of sight.

Galicia is intolerably dreary, battered churches and calvaries, overcast sky, cowed, mediocre, insignificant population. Pitiful people, habituated to all the killing, to soldiers, to disorder, matronly Russian women in tears, rutted roads, stunted grain crops, no sun, Catholic priests with broad hats—but without churches. Deep depression emanates from all those trying to make themselves some sort of life.

The Slavs—the manure of history?

The day passes anxiously. The Poles have broken through the 14th Division's position to our right, and occupied Berestechko again. No information at all, it's a quadrille, they're moving up in our rear.

The mood at HQ. Konstantin Karlovich is silent. The clerks—that gang of insolent, overfed syphilitics—are alarmed. After a hard, monotonous day—a rainy night, mud—I'm wearing low shoes. And this is when the mighty rain sets in, the true victor.

We squelch around in the mud, penetrating fine rain.

Cannon and machine-gun fire nearer all the time. I feel an unbearable urge to sleep. Nothing to give the horses. I have a new coachman—a Pole named Gowiński—a tall, agile, talkative, fussy, and, of course, insolent fellow.

Grishchuk is going home, he explodes sometimes—"I'm tired to death"—he never managed to learn German because his master was a hard man, all they did was quarrel, they never conversed.

It also emerges that he's been starving for seven months, apparently I kept him on short rations.

A Pole—completely barefoot, with a sunken mouth, dark blue eyes. Talkative and cheerful, a renegade, he disgusts me.

An irresistible urge to nod off. Sleeping is dangerous. I lie down fully dressed. Froim's two artificial legs are on a chair beside me. A lamp burning, his black beard, children in a heap on the floor.

I get up ten times—Gowiński and Grishchuk are sleeping—it angers me. I fall asleep toward 4 a.m., a knock at the door—time to be off. Panic, the enemy has reached the town, machine-gun fire, the Poles are getting nearer. Total confusion. They can't get the horses out—they break the doors down, Grishchuk with his revolting despair, there are four of us, the horses haven't been fed, we have to fetch the nurse, Grishchuk and Gowiński want to leave her behind, I yell at them in a voice I don't recognize, "The nurse!" I'm furious—the nurse is stupid, good-looking. We fly along the high road to Brody, I rock and sway and sleep. It's cold, the wind and rain are penetrating. We must watch the horses carefully, the harness is unreliable, the Pole sings, I'm trembling with cold, the nurse is talking nonsense. I sway and sleep. A new sensation—I can't open my eyelids. Describe this inexpressible desire to sleep.

We're on the run from the Poles again. That's cavalry warfare for you, I wake up—we've stopped in front of white buildings. A village? No, Brody.

30 July 1920. Brody

A dismal dawn. Fed up with the nurse. We dropped Grishchuk off somewhere. Godspeed to him.

Where do we go now? My tiredness is getting me down. 6 o'clock in the morning. Some Galician—go to his house. Wife on the floor with a newborn baby. Husband's a quiet old fellow, children with the naked wife, three or four of them.

Some other woman present. Dust, laid by the rain. A cellar. A crucifix. Picture of the Holy Virgin. Uniates really are neither one thing nor the other. A heavy veneer of Catholicism. Bliss—the warmth, a sort of hot stench from the children and women. Silence and melancholy. The nurse is sleeping, I can't, bedbugs. There's no hay, I shout at Gowiński. Our hosts have no bread or milk.

The town has been wrecked, looted. A town of immense interest. Polish culture. An ancient, rich, idiosyncratic Jewish settlement. These horrible markets, dwarves in gaberdines, gaberdines and peyes, old, old men. School Street, nine synagogues, all half-destroyed, I inspect the new synagogue, architecture [two words indecipherable], the shammes, a bearded and talkative Jew—if only there were peace, how good business would be, tells me how the Cossacks plundered the town, the humiliations inflicted by the

Poles. A fine synagogue, how fortunate that at least we have the old stones. This is a Jewish town, this is Galicia, describe it. Trenches, battered factories, Hotel Bristol, waitresses, "Western European" culture—and how greedily you go for it. Those pathetic mirrors, pale Austrian Jews—the owners. And their stories—once we had American dollars, oranges, broadcloth.

The highway, barbed wire, felled trees, and the dreariness, the everlasting dreariness. Nothing to eat, nothing to rely on, war, they're all as bad as the other, equally alien, hostile, savage, where once life was quiet and, most important, replete with tradition.

Budyonny men on the streets. Nothing but watery lemonade in the shops, the barbershops still open. The hags in the market have only carrots, rain all the time, relentless, penetrating, stifling. Unbearable melancholy, people and souls crushed.

At HQ—red trousers, self-confidence, petty souls making themselves important, a horde of young people, some Jews among them, at the personal disposal of the army commander and preoccupied with food.

Must not forget Brody and those pitiful figures—neither the barbers nor the Jews, like visitors from the other world, nor the Cossacks on the streets.

Gowiński is a disaster, no fodder at all for the horses. Halperin's Odessa Hotel, hunger in the town, nothing to eat, good tea in the evening, I try to console my host, he's pale and as panicky as a mouse. Gowiński has found some Poles, got an army cap from them, somebody was willing to help even Gowiński. He is intolerable, doesn't feed the horses, loafs around, jabbers all the time, can't get hold of anything, is afraid he'll be arrested, and they have tried to arrest him, came to see me about it.

Night in the hotel, married couple next door, talking, the words they use, xxxx on the woman's lips, oh you Russians, how disgustingly you spend your nights, and what voices your women have nowadays. I listen with bated breath and am dismayed.

A horrible night in this tormented town of Brody. Must be on the alert. I carry hay to the horses in the night. At HQ. Able to sleep, the enemy is advancing. Went home, slept soundly, numb at heart, Gowiński woke me up.

31 July 1920. Brody, Leszniów

This morning, before leaving, with the tachanka waiting on Golden Street, an hour in a bookshop, a German shop. All sorts of magnificent uncut books, albums, the West, here you have the West, and chivalrous Poland, a chrestomathy, the history of all the Boleslaws, and something tells me that this beauty, this Poland, is so many glittering garments draped around a decrepit body. I rummage among the books like a madman, skim here and there, it's dark, a crowd pours in to loot the stationer's, loathsome young men from the Commission for Captured Enemy Property, with an exaggeratedly martial air. I tear myself away from the shop in despair.

Chrestomathies, Tetmajer, new translations, a mass of new Polish nationalist literature, textbooks.

HQ at Stanisławczyk or Koziuszków. The nurse, she has served with Cheka groups, very Russian, with her soft, bruised beauty. Has lived with all the commissars, I imagine, and suddenly—her Kostroma gymnasium album, the lady schoolteachers, idealistic hearts, the Romanov boarding school, Aunt Manya, skating.

Leszniów yet again, and my former hosts, the dreadful mud, the thin coating of hospitality and respect for Russians has vanished, for all my friendliness, you aren't made to feel very welcome among ruined people.

About the horses, no feed for them, they're getting thin, tachanka buggy is falling to pieces, for trivial reasons I hate Gowiński, that cheerful gluttonous good-for-nothing. They've stopped giving me coffee.

The enemy has bypassed us, pushed us back from the river crossing, sinister rumors that the 14th Division's lines have been breached, dispatch riders galloping around. Toward evening—to Grzymałówka (north of Czurowice)—a ruined village, we got some oats, incessant rain, the short road to HQ impassable in my low shoes, an excruciating journey, our lines are being moved forward, I drank some splendid tea, it's hot, my hostess pretended at first to be ill, the village has been within range of the battle for the crossing throughout. Darkness, anxiety, the Pole is stirring.

Div. commander arrived toward evening, a magnificent figure, gloves, always comes from up front, night at HQ, Konstantin Karlovich's work.

1 August 1920. Grzymałówka, Leszniów

God, it's August, we shall die soon, the ineradicable cruelty of human beings. At the front things are getting worse. Shooting just outside the village. They are pushing us away from the crossing. Everybody has gone, just a few HQ personnel left, my tachanka stands at the door of HQ, I can hear the battle, for some reason I feel good, there are only a few of us, no supply wagons, no administrative staff, life is peaceful, easy, Timoshenko's tremendous composure. Kniga is phlegmatic, Timoshenko: if he doesn't shove them out, I'll have him shot, tell him in so many words, but the div. commander just laughs. The road before us is swollen with rain, machine-gun fire flares up here and there, the invisible presence of the enemy in that gray and shifting sky. The enemy is nearing the village. We are losing the Styr crossing. We ride back to unlucky Leszniów—how many times does that make?

The div. commander joins the 1st Brigade. It's horrible in Leszniów, we are in the place for two hours, the administrative staff is dribbling away, a wall of enemy forces is growing up everywhere.

The battle outside Leszniów. Our infantry in trenches, it's remarkable, young lads from Volhynia, barefoot, semi-idiotic—Russian peasants, and they are actually fighting against Poles, against the gentlemen oppressors. They're short of rifles, the cartridges don't fit, these boys have to skulk in heat-flooded trenches, they get shunted from one forest edge to another. There's a cottage where the forest begins, an obliging Galician makes me tea, the horses stand in a hollow.

I went down to look at a battery, precise, unhurried, technical work.

Under machine-gun fire, whine of bullets, a nasty feeling, we pick our way through the trenches, some Red Army man panics, and of course we are surrounded. Gowiński was up on the road, wanted to abandon the horses, then drove off, I found him at the edge of the forest, the tachanka was wrecked, complications, twists and turns, I look for somewhere to sit, the machine gunners push me down, they are bandaging a wounded lad, leg in the air, he bellows, a friend whose horse has been killed is with him, we strap the tachanka together somehow, ride off, it creaks, won't turn. I have a feeling that Gowiński will be the end of me, he is my fate, his bare belly, the holes in his shoes, his Jewish nose and everlasting excuses. I transfer to Mikhail Karlovich's carriage, what a relief, I doze, evening, I'm in a state of shock, a wagon train, we halt on the road to Bielawce, then follow the road, which is fringed by forest, evening, it's cool, the highroad, sunset—we roll on toward the front line, delivering meat to Konstantin Karlovich.

I am ravenous and wretched. The units are in the forest, they have moved off, the usual picture, the squadron, Bakhturov reads a communiqué about the Third International, how people have assembled from all over the world, I catch glimpses of the nurse's white headscarf between the trees, why is she here? We are going back, what sort of person is Mikhail Karlovich? Gowiński has run away, no horses. Night, I sleep in the carriage beside Mikhail Karlovich. We are outside Bielawce.

Describe the people, the air.

The day is over, I have seen death, white roads, horses under the trees, sunrise and sunset. Above all—Budyonny's men, their horses, troop movements and war, grave, barefoot, spectral Galicians walking through the wheat fields.

Night in the carriage.
(Standing by a little copse with the clerks' tachanka.)

2 August 1920. Bielawce

Trouble with the tachanka. Gowiński approaches the town but of course can't find a smith. My scene with the smith, pushed a woman out of the way, shrieks and tears. The Galicians refuse to fix the thing. I go through the whole arsenal, persuasion, threats, entreaties, a promise of sugar had most effect. A long story, one smith ill, I haul him round to another, more weeping and wailing, he is hauled off home again. They don't want to do my laundry, and nothing will induce them to.

They finally fix it.

I'm tired. Alarm at HQ. We are pulling out. The enemy is putting the pressure on, I run to warn Gowiński, heat, I'm afraid of being too late, run through sand, warn him, catch up with HQ staff outside the village, nobody wants to give me a lift, they leave me behind, I feel miserable. I ride with Barsukov for a while, our destination is Brody.

I am assigned a field ambulance belonging to the 2nd Squadron, we ride up to the forest, halt there with Ivan, my driver. Budyonny and Voroshilov arrive, this will be the decisive battle, not a single step farther. After this all three brigades take up their positions, I speak to the HQ commandant. The atmosphere before the start of battle, a big field, aeroplanes, cavalry maneuvering over the field, our horsemen, explosions in the distance, the battle has begun, machine guns, the sun, the armies have made contact somewhere, a muffled cheer, Ivan and I withdraw, deadly danger, what I feel is not fear, it's passive resignation, he appears to be afraid, where to go, Korochaev's group goes to the right, we for some reason go left, the battle rages, we are overtaken by someone on horseback, a wounded man, deathly pale, "brother, take me with you," his breeches are soaked with blood, he threatens to shoot if we don't take him, we rein in, he is terrifying, blood pours onto Ivan's jacket, a Cossack, we have stopped, I shall bandage him, he has a light wound in the belly, a bone damaged, we pick up another man whose horse has been killed. Describe the wounded man. We wander about the fields for ages, under fire, can't see a thing, these uncaring roads, this scrubby grass, we send out riders, come out onto the highway—where to next, Radziwiłłów or Brody?

The administrative staff and all supply wagons should be in Radziwiłłów, but in my opinion it would be more interesting to go to Brody, for which the battle is being fought. Ivan's opinion prevails, some of the wagoners tell us that the Poles are in Brody, that the supply columns are on the run, that army HQ staff have moved out, so we head for Radziwiłłów. We arrive in the night. All this time we have been eating raw carrots and peas, gnawing hunger, we are dirty, in need of sleep. I choose a cottage on the outskirts of Radziwiłłów. A good guess, I'm acquiring a nose for this sort of thing. An old man, a young girl. Splendid soured milk, we devour it. Tea with milk is made, Ivan goes for sugar, machine-gun fire, clatter of wagons, we rush out, the horse has developed a limp, that's the way it goes, we flee in panic, we are fired on, we can't understand what's happening, he'll catch us any minute now, we charge onto the bridge, milling hordes, we slip into the bog, wild panic, a dead man lying there, abandoned carts, shells, tachankas. Traffic jam, night, terror, wagons at a standstill, endless lines of them, we move on, stop, sleep, stars. What I feel worst about in this whole business is the tea I was deprived of, feel so bad that it seems strange to me. I think about this all night, and hate war.

What a troubled life.

3 August 1920

Night in an open field, we are moving toward Brody in a wagonette. The town keeps changing hands. The same horrifying picture, half in ruins, and the town is waiting for it to happen again. Provisioning point, I meet Barsukov on the outskirts. I ride to HQ. Deserted, dead, dismal. Zotov sleeping on chairs, like a dead man. Borodulin and Pollak also asleep. The Prague Bank building, stripped bare and vandalized, water closets, those tellers' windows, plate glass.

The div. commander is said to be in Klekotów, we spend about two hours in devastated, apprehensive Brody, tea at the barbershop. Ivan waits outside HQ. To go or not to go. We do go, toward Klekotów, turning off the Leszniów highway, no knowing whether Polish forces or our own are there, we are feeling our way, the horses are exhausted, one of them limps more painfully all the time, we eat some potatoes in a village, the brigades suddenly appear, inexplicable beauty, an awesome force advancing, endless ranks, a manorial farm, the manor house in ruins, a thresher, a Clenton traction engine, a tractor, the traction engine still working, it's hot.

The battlefield, I meet the div. commander, where is HQ staff, we have lost Zholnarkevich. The battle begins, artillery cover, explosions quite near, a fearful moment, the decisive battle—will we halt the Polish advance or won't we, Budyonny to Kolesnikov and Grishin—"I'll shoot you," they go away white-faced, on foot.

Before that—the dreadful field, sown with mangled men, inhuman cruelty, unbelievable wounds, fractured skulls, naked young bodies gleaming white in the sun, jettisoned notebooks, leaflets, soldiers' books, Bibles, bodies amid the wheat.

My mind rather than my eyes receives these impressions. The battle begins, I am given a horse, I see the columns form up, they advance to attack, I feel sorry for these unfortunates, no people, just columns, the firing reaches its maximum intensity, then the butcher's work is carried out, wordlessly. I ride on, rumors that the div. commander has been recalled?

The beginning of my adventures, I make for the highway with the supply wagons, the fighting gets fiercer, I find a provisioning point under fire on the highway, shells whistling past, explosions twenty paces away, feeling of hopelessness, the wagons leave at a gallop, I tag on to the 20th Regiment, 4th Division, wounded men, cantankerous commander, no, he says, I'm not wounded, just got a knock, we're professionals, and nothing but fields, sun, corpses, I sit by the field kitchen, hunger, dried peas, no fodder for the horses. The field kitchen, conversation, we are sitting on the grass, the regiment suddenly moves out, I need to go toward Radziwiłłów, the regiment is going in the direction of Leszniów, I have no strength left, am afraid of being separated. An endless journey, dusty roads, I change over to a cart, Quasimodo, two donkeys, a gruesome spectacle—that hunchbacked driver, taciturn, with a face as dark as the forests of Murom.

We ride on, I have an awful feeling I'm getting farther and farther from the division. I cherish one hope—that afterward we shall be able to take the wounded man to Radziwiłłów, the wounded man has a pale Jewish face.

We ride into the woods, gunfire, shells a hundred paces away, wander endlessly around the fringes of the forest.

The sand is sticky, difficult to move in. Poem about cruelly overworked horses.

An apiary, we search the hives, four huts in the forest, nothing there, everything stolen, I ask a Red Army man for bread, he says "I don't have anything to do with Jews," I'm an outsider, in long trousers, I don't belong, I'm all alone, we ride on, I'm so tired I can hardly sit on my horse, I have to look after it myself, we ride into Koniuszków, we steal some barley, they tell me to look around and take what I can, take the lot, I look around the village for a nurse, women in hysterics, five minutes after our arrival the looting starts, women struggling, weeping and wailing, it's unbearable, I can't stand these never-ending horrors, I go looking for a nurse, I feel unbearably sad, I pinch a mug of milk from the regimental commander, snatch a flatcake out of the hands of a peasant woman's little boy.

Ten minutes later we ride out. Just like that! The Poles are somewhere around. Back we go again, I think I won't be able to stand it, at a trot, what's more, I ride first with the commander, then attach myself to the supply wagons, I try to get a seat on a cart, the answer is always the same—the horses are on their last legs, all right—knock me off and sit here, come on, dear boy, sit here, only we've got dead men in here, I look under some sacking, there are dead bodies.

We come to a field, there are many supply wagons belonging to the 4th Division, an artillery battery, another field kitchen, I look for nurses, a grim night, I want to sleep, I must feed the horse, I lie down, the horses are cropping the splendid wheat, Red Army men in the wheat, pale, dead to the world. The horse is a nuisance to me, I chase after it, I join up with a nurse, we sleep in the buggy, the nurse is old, bald, probably Jewish, a martyr, this intolerable swearing, the driver tries to push her off, the horses wander at random, you can't keep the driver awake, he is rude and swears at us, she says "our heroes are horrible people." She covers him up, they sleep with their arms around each other, that unhappy old nurse. I'd like to shoot the driver, all that nagging and swearing, the nurse is not of this world—we fall asleep. I wake up two hours later—the bridle has been stolen. Despair. Daybreak. We are seven versts from Radziwiłłów. I ride on following my nose. Unhappy horse, we are all unhappy, the regiment is going on farther. I set off again.

For this day—the main thing is to describe the Red Army men and the air.

4 August 1920

I am traveling alone toward Radziwiłłów. It's hard going. No one else going my way, the horse has slowed down, every step I take I'm afraid I may meet the Poles. I got away with it, Polish units in the Radziwiłłow area, gloom and confusion in the town, they tell me to go to the station, the population is stripped bare, and used by now to all the changes. Sheko in an automobile. I am in Budyonny's quarters. A Jewish family, young ladies, a group from the Bukhteev gymnasium, Odessa, my heart stands still.

Oh happiness, they give me cocoa and bread. News—the new

div. commander is Apanasenko, the new div. chief of staff—Sheko. Wonders will never cease.

Zholnarkevich arrives with his squadron, he is pitiable, Zotov informs him that he has been replaced, I'll go and sell biscuits on the Sukharevka, he says, that's the new school for you, he says, you know how to deploy troops, I used to in the old days, but I can't do it now, with no reserves.

He's feverish, says things he ought not to say, squabbles with Sheko, Sheko immediately gets high and mighty, says the chief of staff has ordered you to report to HQ, I'm not going to sit any exams, he says, I'm not a schoolboy to go wasting my time with staff officers, leaves his squadron and rides off. The old guard is pulling out, everything is falling to pieces now Konstantin Karlovich is gone.

Another impression—as painful as it is unforgettable—the arrival of the div. commander on a white horse, with dispatch riders. All the HQ riffraff, running around with chickens under their arms for the army commander, their patronizing attitude, insolence. Sheko is arrogant, asks about operations, the div. commander explains, smiles, a magnificent, imposing figure, desperation. Yesterday's fighting—the 6th Division's brilliant success, 1,000 horses, three regiments driven into the trenches, the enemy shattered, repulsed, div. HQ in Khotin. Whose victory—Timoshenko's or Apanasenko's? Comrade Khmelnitsky—a Jew, greedy-guts, coward, insolent, in front of the army commander—a chicken, a piglet, corn, the dispatch riders despise him, those insolent dispatch riders, their sole concern is chickens, fatback, they stuff themselves, they're all fat, the drivers all stuff themselves with fatback, all this out on the porch in front of the building. Nothing for my horse to eat.

The mood changes completely, the Poles are retreating, although they are occupying Brody, we're hitting them again, Budyonny has pulled us through.

I want to sleep, but can't. The changes in the life of the division will have important consequences. Sheko in a cart. I'm with the squadron. We are making for Khotin again at a gallop, have done 15 versts. I'm living with Bakhturov. He is half dead, the div. commander is no longer here, and he feels that he won't be here much longer either. The division is in a state of shock, the soldiers move gingerly—will it heal or won't it. I've had some supper at last—meat, honey. Describe Bakhturov, Ivan Ivanovich, and Petro. I sleep in a barn, peace at last.

5 August 1920. Khotin

A day of peace and quiet. I eat, wander around the sun-washed village, we all rest, I've had dinner and supper—there's honey, milk.

The main thing—internal changes, everything is upside down.

I feel so sorry for the div. commander it hurts, the Cossacks are uneasy, a lot of talking behind backs, an interesting phenomenon, they get together and whisper, Bakhturov is despondent, the div. commander was a hero, now the new commander won't even let him into the room, 6,000 instead of 600, a grave humiliation, they flung it in his face—you're a traitor, Timoshenko burst out laughing—Apanasenko, a new and striking figure, ugly, uncouth, hotheaded, egotistical, ambitious, appealed to Stavropol and the Don about disorder in the rear, just to let his native place know that he is a div. commander. Timoshenko was easier, jollier, more broad-minded, and perhaps worse. Two different men, they probably never liked each other. Sheko is coming on strong, incredibly garbled orders, arrogance. Work at HQ has changed completely. No supply wagons, no administrative staff. Lepin has raised his head—he's angry, stupid, argues with Sheko.

In the evening music and dancing, Apanasenko is courting popularity, his circle is widening, he picks one of the captured Polish horses for Bakhturov, everybody rides a Polish horse now, they are splendid horses, narrow-chested, tall, English, reddish brown, unforgettable. Apanasenko has the horses paraded.

All day long—talk about intrigues. Letter to the rear.

Homesick for Odessa.

Remember—Apanasenko's figure, his face, his joyousness, his love of horses, how he paraded the horses to choose one for Bakhturov.

About the dispatch riders who hitch their fortunes to those of their "masters." What will Mikheev do, or lame Sukhorukov, all those Grebushkas, Tarasovs, and Ivan Ivanovich with Bakhturov. They all follow blindly.

About Polish horses, about the squadrons, galloping through the dust on tall, golden, narrow-chested Polish horses. Topknots, chains, clothes made out of rugs. 600 horses got stuck in the bog, unlucky Poles.

6 August 1920. Khotin

Same place. We put ourselves in order, shoe the horses, eat, a pause in operations.

My landlady is a small, fragile, timid woman with meek, tormented eyes. God, how the soldiers torment her, the never-ending cook-up, we steal her honey. Her husband has come home, bombs from an aeroplane frightened his horses away. The old man hasn't eaten for five days, now he's off to look for his horses up hill and down dale, it's an epic. An old, old man.

A sultry day, heavy white silence, my heart is glad, the horses stand resting, oats are threshed for them, the Cossacks sleep the day away beside them, the horses are resting, that's the main thing.

I catch glimpses of Apanasenko, unlike the reserved Timoshenko he is one of us, our fatherly commander.

Bakhturov left this morning, with his retinue, I watch the new military commissar at work, a Moscow workingman, obtuse but with the rough edges rubbed off, the way to be strong—follow the well-trodden highways, three commissars, must describe limpy Gubanov the terror of the regiment, a reckless roughneck, a youngster of 23, then there's modest Shiryaev and crafty Grishin. They sit in the little garden, the military commissar asks questions, they gossip, talk grandiloquently about world revolution, the landlady tries shaking down apples, they've all been eaten up, the commissar's secretary, a lanky fellow with a ringing voice, walks around looking for food.

New currents at HQ—Sheko writing special orders, pretentious and high-flown, but brief and forceful, offers the Revolutionary War Council his views, acts on his own initiative.

Everyone mourns Timoshenko's departure, but there will be no mutiny.

Why can't I get over my sadness? Because I'm far from home, because we are destroyers, because we move like a whirlwind, like a stream of lava, hated by everyone, life shatters, I am at a huge, never-ending service for the dead.

Ivan Ivanovich sits on a bench and talks about the days when he could spend 20 or 30 thousand at a go. They all have gold, they helped themselves to it in Rostov, slung sacks full of money over their saddles and took off. Ivan Ivanovich used to keep women, buy them dresses. Night, the barn, fragrant hay, but the air is heavy, and I'm oppressed by something, perhaps the sad senselessness of my life.

7 August 1920. Berestechko

It's evening now, 8. Lamps have just been lit in the town. Prayers for the dead in the next room. Many Jews, familiar doleful chants, they sway as they sing, sitting on benches, two candles, an eternal lamp on the windowsill. It's a service for our host's granddaughter, who died of fright after the looting. Her mother weeps while the prayers are said, talks to me—we are standing by the table—says she has been "threshed" by grief for two months now. She shows us a photograph, worn thin by tearstains, and everyone says she was an extraordinary beauty, some commander had gone berserk, a knock in the night, they were routed out of bed, the Poles ransacked the place, then the Cossacks, she couldn't stop vomiting, wasted away. The main thing the Jews kept saying—she was a beauty, the like of whom the town had never seen.

A memorable day. In the morning—from Khotin to Berestechko. I ride with Ivanov, the commissar's secretary, a lanky, glutonous young fellow with no backbone, a ragamuffin and would you believe it, the husband of Komarova, the singer, "we used to do concerts together, I'm going to send for her." A Russian maenad.

Corpse of a murdered Pole, a terrifying corpse, swollen and naked, grotesque.

Berestechko has changed hands several times. Historic fields outside Berestechko, Cossack graves. The most striking thing is how everything repeats itself—Cossack against Pole, more often still—peasant against Polish landlord.

I won't forget this town with its long, narrow, roofed-in stinking courtyards, all of it 100–200 years old, its population sturdier than in other places, above all, the architecture, white and watery-blue little houses, lanes, synagogues, peasant women. Life is slowly returning to normal. Life here used to be worth living, a solid Jewish community, rich Ukrainians, market on Sundays, a unique class of Russian urban artisans, leather workers, trade with Austria, smuggling.

The Jews here are less fanatical, better dressed, more robust, you could even say jollier, very old men, gaberdines, old women, everything is redolent of olden times, tradition, the town is steeped in the bloody history of the Polish-Jewish ghetto. Hatred for the Poles is unanimous. They have looted, tortured, branded the pharmacist with a red-hot iron, put needles under his nails, pulled out his hair, all because somebody shot at a Polish officer. What idiocy. The Poles have gone mad, they are destroying themselves.

An ancient Catholic church, graves of Polish officers in the churchyard, fresh mounds, ten days old, white birchwood crosses, all this is horrible, the priest's house has been destroyed, I find ancient books, precious Latin manuscripts. The priest was called Tuzinkiewicz. I find a photograph of him, short and fat, labored here 45 years, lived in the same place, a scholastic, a varied collection of books, many in Latin. 1860 editions, that's when Tuzinkiewicz really lived, huge old-fashioned living quarters, dark pictures, photographs of church dignitaries assembled in Zhitomir, portraits of Pope Pius X, a nice face, an amazing portrait of Sienkiewicz—there he is, the essence of a nation. And over all this the stink of Sukhin's miserable little soul. How new all this is to me—the books, the soul of a Catholic pater, a Jesuit, I try to capture the soul and heart of Tuzinkiewicz, and succeed. Lepin suddenly starts playing the piano, movingly. He sings sometimes in Latvian. Remember his little bare feet—you could die laughing. A very comical creature.

A dreadful incident, the church was sacked, vestments torn up, precious, shimmering fabrics in tatters, on the floor, the nurse made off with three bales, linings were ripped open, candles stolen, chests staved in, papal bulls thrown out, money pocketed, a magnificent church, 200 years old, the things it's seen (Tuzinkiewicz's manuscripts), so many counts and serfs, magnificent Italian paintings, rosy priests rocking the infant Christ, a magnificent dark Christ, Rembrandt, a Madonna in the manner of Murillo, maybe it is a Murillo, and above all those well-nourished, saintly Jesuits, an eerie, miniature Chinese figure behind a veil, wearing a raspberry-colored Polish frock coat, a bearded little Jew, a bench, a shattered shrine, the statue of St. Valentine. The verger quivers like a bird, writhes, speaks a mixture of Russian and Polish, I'm not allowed to touch it he sobs. "They're wild beasts, they've come to wreck and rob, it's obvious, the old gods are being destroyed."

Evening in the town. The church is closed. In the late afternoon I visit the castle of the counts Raciborowski. An old man of 70 and his 90-year-old mother. There were just the two of them, both mad, so the locals say. Describe this pair. Ancient, aristocratic Polish house, probably more than 100 years old, bright, old-fashioned paintings on the ceilings, remains of antlers, small rooms for the servants up above, flagstones, passageways, excrement on the floor, little Jewish boys, a Steinway piano, sofas ripped open, springs sticking out, remember the doors, light white doors, oak doors, letters in French dated 1820, "notre petit héros achève 7 semaines." God, who can have written them, and when, these trampled letters, I pick up some relics, a century ago, the mother a countess, a Steinway, the park, an artificial lake.

I can't tear myself away—I think of Hauptmann, of Elga.

Public meeting in the castle park, the Jews of Berestechko, obtuse Vinokurov, children running around, a Revolutionary Committee is being elected, the Jewish men finger their beards, Jewish women listen to what's said about the Russian paradise, the international situation, the rising in India.

An unquiet night, we were told to be on the alert, alone with the decrepit m'shores, his surprising eloquence, what was he talking about?

8 August 1920. Berestechko

I'm beginning to feel at home in this town. They used to have market fairs here. The peasants sell pears. The money they get paid in has long ceased to be legal tender. The place used to be a hive of activity—the Jews used to export grain to Austria, goods and people were smuggled across the nearby frontier.

Unusual barns, cellars.

I am lodging with the proprietress of an inn, a skinny redheaded old bag. Ilchenko has bought some cucumbers, is reading *Everybody's Magazine* and holding forth on economic policy, says the Jews are to blame for everything, an obtuse Slav creature, stuffed his pockets when Rostov was sacked. Some foster children, mother recently dead. The story of the pharmacist, the Poles stuck pins under his fingernails, insane people.

A hot day, people loitering about coming to life again, they'll start trading soon.

The synagogue, Torah scrolls, built 36 years ago by a craftsman from Kremenets, he was paid 50 rubles a month, golden peacocks, folded hands, ancient Torah scrolls, not one shammes shows any enthusiasm, moth-eaten old men, the bridges into Berestechko, how they swayed, the Poles gave the whole place a distinctive character which it has long lost. The little old man with whom Korochaev, the demoted div. commander, lodged, with his Jewish henchman. Korochaev used to be chairman of the Cheka somewhere in Astrakhan, prod him and it all comes pouring out. Making friends with the Jew. We drink tea at the old man's. Quiet, good-humored. I roam around the town, life goes on in the Jewish hovels—wretched, powerful, immortal—young women in white stockings, shifts, how few fat people there are here.

We are reconnoitering in the direction of Lvov, Apanasenko writes epistles to the Stavropol Executive Committee, "We shall be cutting off heads in the rear," he's delighted with himself. A battle at Radziechów, Apanasenko acquits himself like a hero—lightening-quick deployment of his troops, very nearly had the 14th Division shot for retreating. We are approaching Radziechów.

Moscow newspapers dated 29 July. Opening of the Second Congress of the Third International, unification of the peoples finally realized, now all is clear: there are two worlds, and war between them is declared. We will fight on endlessly. Russia has thrown down the gauntlet. We shall advance into Europe and conquer the world. The Red Army has become a factor of world significance.

Must take a closer look at Apanasenko. An ataman.

The quiet old man's memorial service for his granddaughter.

Evening, a theatrical performance in the count's garden, amateurs from Berestechko, the doltish orderly, young ladies from Berestechko, things are quieting down, I should like to stay here awhile and learn more.

9 August 1920. Łaszków

The move from Berestechko to Łaszków. Galicia. The div. commander's carriage, the div. commander's dispatch rider Lyovka—the one who trades and races horses. Tells a story about whipping his neighbor Stepan, who had been a village policeman under Denikin, ill-treated the locals, and returned to the village. They wouldn't let anyone kill him outright, they beat him up in jail, slit his back open, jumped on him, danced on him, and an epic conversation took place. Does that feel nice, Stepan? Awful. And those you mistreated, did it feel nice to them? It was awful. Did you think it would be awful for you someday? No, I didn't. Well, you should have, Stepan, we here think that if we'd got caught you'd have cut our throats, sure you would, so now we're going to kill you, Stepan. They left him barely warm. Another story about Shurka, the nurse. Night, a battle, the regiments are forming up, Lyovka in a phaeton, Shurka's bedfellow is badly wounded, gives Lyovka his horse, they remove the wounded man, go back to the battle. Come on, Shura, you only live once, and only die once. Oh, all right. She went to school in Rostov, gallops with the regiment, she can give anybody fifteen. Right, Shura, off we go, we'll retreat now, the horses were getting tangled in the wire, he rides four versts, a village, he squats, cuts the wire, the regiment goes through, Shura leaves the ranks, Lyovka makes supper, they're ravenous, they eat a bit, talk a bit, come on, Shura, let's be having it, just once more. Well, all right. But where?

She gallops off after the regiment, he goes off somewhere to sleep. If your wife turns up I'll kill her.

Łaszków is a green, sunny, quiet, prosperous Galician village. I am lodging with the deacon. His wife has just given birth. Dispirited people. A clean, new cottage, with nothing in it. The neighbors typical Galician Jews. They wonder whether I'm Jewish. Their story—looters, one cut off the heads of two hens, found things hidden in the barn, dug them up, drove everybody into the cottage, the usual story, must remember the lad with the sideburns. They tell me the chief rabbi lives in Bełz, most of the rabbis have been exterminated.

We are resting. The 1st Squadron is in my fenced garden. Night, I have a small lamp on my table, horses are quietly snorting, they're all Kuban Cossacks here, they eat together, sleep together, cook together, a splendid silent comradeship. They are all more or less peasants, in the evening they sing songs that sound like church music in lusty voices, their devotion to horses, beside each man a little heap—saddle, bridle, ornamented saber, greatcoat, I sleep in the midst of them.

In the daytime I sleep out in the open. No military operations, what a beautiful and necessary thing is rest. The cavalry and its horses recuperate after their inhuman toil, men take a healing rest from cruelty, living together, singing quietly, telling each other stories.

HQ is in the school building. The div. commander is in the priest's house.

10 August 1920. Łaszków

Our rest continues. Reconnaissance in the direction of Radziechów, Sokołówka, Stojanów, all on the way to Lvov. We get the news that Aleksandrovsk has been taken, gigantic complications in the international situation, surely we're not going to be at war with the whole world?

A fire in the village. The priest's barn burns down. Two horses thrash around with all the strength that's in them, but perish in the blaze. You can't lead a horse out of a fire. Two cows ran away, the hide of one of them cracked, blood poured out of the cracks, it was moving, pitiful.

The whole village is enveloped in smoke, bright flame, fat black clouds of smoke, a mass of wood, the heat on my face, everything carried out of the priest's house and the church, thrown into the garden. Apanasenko in a red, knee-length pleated coat and a black felt cloak, close-shaven—a fearsome apparition, an ataman.

Our Cossacks, a depressing spectacle, stealing things from the back porch, their eyes smarting, all looking sheepish, it's ineradicable, this so-called force of habit. All the banners, an ancient Chet'i-Minei, icons carried out, strange images painted pink and white or blue and white, ugly, flat-faced, Chinese or Buddhist, a mass of paper flowers, will the church catch fire, peasant women silently wring their hands, the villagers frightened and silent, run around barefoot, every householder sits by his cottage with a bucket. They are apathetic, beaten down, numbed—it's extraordinary, they should be rushing to put the fire out. We've managed to control the thieving—soldiers slink around the priest's cases like thwarted beasts of prey, tell each other there's gold there, it's all right to take anything belonging to a priest, a portrait of Count Andrzej Szeptycki, Metropolitan of Galicia. A valiant magnate with a black ring on his large, aristocratic hand. The old priest has served 35 years in Łaszków, lower lip never stops trembling, tells me about Szeptycki who "wasn't educated in the Polish spirit," from a family of Ruthenian grandees, "the counts of Szeptycki," who afterward went over to the Poles, his brother is a commander in chief of the Polish armed forces, but Andrzej had returned to his Ruthenians. The priest's old-world culture, quiet and assured. A nice intelligent priest who has laid in a supply of flour, some chickens, a hen, he wants to talk about universities, unlucky man, he has Apanasenko in his red Cossack coat living in the house.

Night—an unusual spectacle, the highroad burning brightly in the last rays, my room is lit up, I'm working, the lamp is lit, peace and quiet, the Kuban Cossacks are singing sentimentally, their slim forms in the light of camp fires, the songs are just like Ukrainian ones, the horses lie down to sleep. I go to the div. commander's. I hear stories about him from Vinokurov—a partisan, an ataman, a rebel, Cossack freedom, a wild uprising, his ideal is Dumenko, an open wound, must subordinate yourself to an organization, deadly hatred of the aristocracy, the priests and, above all, the intelligentsia, whose presence in the army he can't stomach. He'll graduate from an institute—Apanasenko, how is it different from the times of Bogdan Khmelnitsky?

Middle of the night. 4 a.m.

11 August 1920. Łaszków

A day of work, sitting at HQ writing till I'm too tired, and of rest. Rain toward evening. Cossacks spending the night in my room, strange—both peaceable and warlike, housebroken, not particularly young peasants of obvious Ukrainian extraction.

About the Kuban Cossacks. A community of comrades, always keep to themselves, horses snorting under my window night and day, glorious smell of dung, of sunshine, of sleeping Cossacks, twice a day they cook huge cauldrons of soup, and meat. At night I have Cossack visitors. Incessant rain, they dry out and eat their supper in my room. The religious Cossack in the soft hat, pale face, fair moustache. They are serious, friendly, wild but somehow more attractive, more domesticated, less foul-mouthed, more peaceable than the Don Cossacks and those from Stavropol.

The nurse has arrived, how clear it all is, I must describe it, she is worn to a frazzle, wants to get away, everybody's been there—the commander, or so at least they say, Yakovlev and, horror of horrors, Gusev. She is pitiful, wants to leave, sad, speaks incoherently, tries to talk to me and looks at me with trusting eyes, as much as to say you're my friend, and the others, the others are slime. How quickly they've destroyed a human being, degraded her, made her ugly. She is naive, stupid, susceptible, even to revolutionary catchphrases— the silly girl talks about revolution a lot, once worked in the Culture and Education section of the Cheka, so many masculine influences.

Interview with Apanasenko. Very interesting. This I must remember. His obtuse, terrible face, his powerful, stocky frame, just like Utochkin's.

His dispatch riders (Lyovka), graceful golden horses, his hangers-on, carriages, his adopted son Volodya—a diminutive Cossack with an old man's face, swears like a grown-up.

Apanasenko is hungry for fame, here it is—the new class. Whatever the battle plans—he breaks away and is back where he started, an organizer of task forces, simply hostile to officers, 4 George Crosses, a martinet, NCO, ensign in Kerensky's time, chairman of the regimental committee, stripped officers of their epaulets, long months in the Astrakhan steppes, incontestable authority, a professional soldier.

About the atamans, there were many of them around, they got hold of machine guns, fought with Shkuro and Mamontov, merged with the Red Army, a heroic epic. This isn't a Marxist revolution, it's a Cossack rebellion, out to win all and lose nothing. Apanasenko's hatred of the rich, of the intelligentsia, an unquenchable hatred.

Night with the Kuban Cossacks, rain, stuffy, I have some sort of peculiar itch.

12 August 1920. Łaszków

Our fourth day in Łaszków. A more than usually cowed Galician village. They used to live better than Russians, good houses, strong sense of order, respect for priests, honest people but bloodless, the scalded child of my hosts, how and why he was born, his mother has not a drop of blood left, they keep hiding things anywhere and everywhere, I can hear pigs grunting, they probably have cloth hidden somewhere.

A free day, a good thing—my newspaper work, mustn't neglect it.

Also write for the newspaper a biography of Apanasenko.

The division is resting—a sort of hush in the heart, and people nicer—songs, camp fires, fire in the night, jokes, happy, apathetic horses, someone reads a newspaper, men amble lazily, horses are being shod. What all this looks like. Sokolov is going on leave, I give him a letter home.

I am writing—a lot about pipes, about long-forgotten things, never mind the Revolution, that's what one should concentrate on.

Mustn't forget the priest at Łaszków, unshaven, good-natured, educated, perhaps mercenary, but mercenary is hardly the word— just a hen, a duck, his house, he used to live comfortably, comic etchings.

Friction between the military commissar and the div. commander, he got up and left with Kniga while Yakovlev, the divisional political commissar, was giving a report, Apanasenko had come to see the commissar.

Vinokurov is a typical military commissar, he sticks to a line of his own, wants to reform the 6th Division, the struggle with the partisan mentality, slow-witted, bores me to death with his speeches, rude at times, addresses everyone familiarly.

13 August 1920. Niwice

Orders came in the night—advance on Busk, 35 versts east of Lvov.

We move out in the morning. All three brigades concentrated in the same place. I am on Misha's horse, it has learned to gallop, but won't go at walking pace, terrible trotter. On horseback all day with the div. commander. The farm at Porady. In the forest, four enemy planes, volley fire. Three brigade commanders, Kolesnikov, Korochaev, Kniga. Vasili Ivanovich's cunning move, made as if to bypass Toporów (Chanyz) no contact with the enemy. We are on a farm at Porady, ruined cottages. I extract an old woman from a hatch under the floor, stuffed cabbage. With the gunnery observer at a battery. We attack near a copse.

A disaster—marshlands, ditches, no room for the cavalry to maneuver, attack in infantry formation, halfheartedly, is our morale sagging? The battle outside Toporów, stubborn, yet easy (in comparison with the imperialist bloodbath), they attack on three sides, cannot prevail, hurricane of artillery fire from two of our batteries.

Night. All our attacks have failed. Overnight HQ moves to Niwice. Thick mist, penetrating cold, the horse, the road runs through the forest, camp fires and candles, nurses in buggies, a difficult journey after a day of alarms ending in failure.

Over fields and through forests all day long. Most interesting of all is the div. commander, his mocking laugh, his swearing, his abrupt exclamations, snorts of disgust, shrugs, his agitation, responsibility for all that has happened, passionate belief that if only he had been there all would have been well.

What remains in my memory? The night ride, the screams of women at Porady when they began (I stopped writing here, two bombs exploded 100 paces away, dropped from an aeroplane. We are on the edge of the forest to the west of Stary Majdan) taking their linen, our attack, something we can't quite make out, not alarming at a distance, patrols of some sort, horsemen crossing a meadow, from far off it's unclear why any of this is being done, and not at all frightening.

When we got right up to the town, things heated up, the moment of attack, the moment when a town may be taken, the nerve-racking, feverish, ever-louder chatter of machine guns driving you to desperation, the incessant explosions, and up above—silence, nothing to be seen.

Apanasenko's staff at work—hourly reports to the army commander, he's looking for a commendation.

We arrived at Niwice chilled to the bone and tired. Warm kitchen. A schoolhouse.

The teacher's captivating wife, a nationalist, a sort of inner merriment about her, asks questions, makes us tea, stands up for her language—your *mowa* is good and so is our mowa, all with laughter in her eyes. And this in Galicia, it's good, it's so long since I heard anything like it. I sleep in the classroom, on straw, beside Vinokurov.

I've got a cold.

14 August 1920

Focus of operations—take Busk and cross the Bug. Attacking Toporów all day long, no, we've pulled back. Another indecisive day. The forest edge at Stary Majdan. The enemy has taken Łopatyn.

We drive them out toward evening. Niwice again. Lodge overnight with an old woman, in the yard with the staff.

15 August 1920

In Toporów in the morning. Fighting near Busk. HQ is in Busk. Trying to force our way across the Bug. There's a big fire on the other side. Budyonny is in Busk.

Spend the night at Jabłonówka with Vinokurov.

16 August 1920

To Rakobuty, a brigade made it across.

I go to interrogate prisoners.

Back in Jabłonówka. We move on toward Nowy Milatyn and Stary Milatyn, panic, spend the night in an almshouse.

17 August 1920

Fighting near the railroad track at Liski. Massacre of prisoners. Spend the night in Zadworze.

18 August 1920

Had no time to write. We have moved on. Since we started out on 13 Aug. we have been on the move the whole time, endless roads, the squadron's pennant, Apanasenko's horses, skirmishes, farms, corpses. Frontal assault on Toporów, Kolesnikov goes in to the attack, marshy ground, I am at an observation point, toward evening hurricane of fire from two batteries. The Polish infantry stays put in the trenches, our troops advance, return, horse holders guide the wounded, Cossacks don't like frontal attacks, smoke over the damned trench. That was on the 13th. On the 14th the division moved toward Busk, had to reach it at any price, by evening was ten versts away. That's where the main operation—crossing the Bug—must be carried out. We are simultaneously looking for a ford.

Czech farm at Adamy, breakfast in the farmhouse, potatoes and milk, Sukhorukov, at home under all regimes, ass-licker, Suslov and all the Lyovkas sing his tune. Main impressions—dark forests, wagon trains in the forest, candlelight falling on the nurses, rumbling, the tempos of troops on the move. We are on the fringe of the forest, the horses are grazing, the heroes of the day are the aeroplanes, air operations are increasing steadily, an air attack, they fly over 5 or 6 at a time, bombs 100 paces away, I have an ashgray gelding, horrible horse. In the forest. Hanky-panky with the nurse. Apanasenko came straight out with a disgusting proposal, she is supposed to have slept with him, now speaks of him with loathing, but fancies Sheko, and is herself fancied by the divisional military commissar, who disguises his interest in her as something else, says she's defenseless, no transport, no one to protect her. She tells us how Konstantin Karlovich once courted her, gave her food, forbade people to write letters to her, but they kept on endlessly writing. She found Yakovlev terribly attractive—head of the Registration Department, a fair-haired youngster in a red cap, asked for her hand and her heart, sobbing like a child. There was some other story, but I couldn't find out anything about it. It's a whole epic, the nurse's story—mainly there's a lot of gossip about her, everyone despises her, her own driver won't talk to her, her ankle boots, little aprons, she gives little presents, pamphlets of Bebel.

Woman and Socialism.

A whole volume could be written on women in the Red Army. The squadrons go into battle, dust, din, bared sabers, furious cursing, and they gallop forward with their skirts tucked up, covered in dust, with their big breasts, all whores, but comrades, whores because they're comrades, that's what matters, they're there to serve everybody, in any way they can, heroines, and at the same time despised, they water the horses, tote hay, mend harness, steal from the churches and from the civilian population.

Apanasenko's irritability, his swearing—is this what's meant by strength of will?

Night in Niwice again, sleep on straw, anywhere, because I can't think any more, my clothes are in shreds, my body aches, ONE HUNDRED versts on horseback.

Spend the night with Vinokurov. His relations with Ivanov. What am I to make of this pathetic, greedy, tall young man with his soft voice, his limp soul, and his keen mind? The military commissar is intolerably rude to him, curses him incessantly, picks on every little thing, what d'you think you're doing, then some filthy language, don't know, eh, haven't done it, eh, get your gear together, I'm kicking you out.

I must look deeply into the soul of the fighting man, I am trying to, but it's all horrible, wild beasts with principles.

The 2nd Brigade has taken Toporów in an attack by night. An unforgettable morning. We move at a brisk trot. A dreadful, an eerie town, Jews in their doorways look like corpses, how much more can happen to you, I think, black beards, bent backs, ruined homes, there's [illegible], remnants of German order and comfort, indescribable—that resigned, burning Jewish sadness. There is also a monastery. Apanasenko is radiant. The 2nd Brigade rides through. Topknots, clothes made out of rugs, red tobacco pouches, short carbines, their commanders on imposing horses, a Budyonny brigade. A ride-past, bands playing, greetings, sons of the Revolution, Apanasenko radiant.

On from Toporów—forest, roads, HQ staff by the roadside, dispatch riders, brigade commanders, we fly into Busk at a quick trot, into its eastern half. What an enchanting place (this is on the 18th, a plane overhead, will start bombing any minute now), pure Jewish women, orchards full of pears and plums, brilliant noonday, curtains, remnants of clean and perhaps honest petit-bourgeois ordinariness in the houses, mirrors, we are lodging with a fat Galician woman, widow of a teacher, wide sofas, lots of plums, unbearable tiredness from tension (shell flew over, didn't explode), couldn't get to sleep, lay by a wall next to the horses and remembered the dust of the road and the horror of the milling supply wagons, dust is the most awe-inspiring phenomenon of our war.

Fighting in Busk on the other side of the bridge. Our wounded. Beauty—the town burning over there. I ride to the crossing—acutely aware of the battle, have to run part of the way, because the enemy has it under fire, night, lit up by burning buildings, horses stand close to the cottages, Budyonny is conferring, the Revolutionary Military Council comes out, a sense of danger, they haven't taken Busk head on, we say goodbye to the fat Galician woman and ride to Jabłonówka in the dead of night, the horses can hardly move, we spend the night in a hole, on straw, the div. commander has left, the military commissar and I haven't the strength to go farther.

The 1st Brigade has found a ford and crossed the Bug at Podburzany. Morning—to the crossing point with Vinokurov. And there it is, the Bug, a shallow little river, the staff up on a hill, I am worn out by the journey, but they send me back to Jabłonówka to interrogate prisoners. Calamity. Describe the feelings of a rider: weariness, his horse won't go, he has a long way to ride, he is exhausted, the scorched steppe, loneliness, no one to help, versts to infinity.

Interrogating prisoners at Jabłonówka. People in their underwear, some Jews among them, little fair-haired Poles, exhausted, an educated youngster, sullen hatred for them, a wounded man's blood-soaked underwear, no water given to them, some ugly customer sticks papers in my hand. You're lucky, I think, to get off so lightly. They surround me, they are delighted by the sound of my benevolent voice, miserable dust, what a difference between the Cossacks and these people, delicate creatures.

I return from Jabłonówka to HQ in a tachanka. Ford the river again, endless wagon trains crossing (they never delay a minute, right behind the advancing units), they sink into the river, traces snap, the dust is suffocating, Galician villages, I am given milk, in one village a meal, the Poles have only just withdrawn, all is quiet, the village is numb, the heat, the noonday silence, no one in the village, amazing—such an untroubled silence, such light, such peace, in this place, the front could be at least 100 versts away. The churches in the villages.

Farther on—the enemy. Two butchered Poles, naked, their small faces slashed to pieces, shining through the rye in the sunlight.

We return to Jabłonówka, tea with Lepin, dirt, Cherkashin humiliates him and wants to drop him, if you look closely Cherkashin has a terrible face, in that tall figure, straight as a ramrod, you sense the peasant underneath—drunkard, thief, and cunning rogue.

Lepin—dirty, dull, touchy, incomprehensible.

Long, interminable story told by handsome Bazkunov, his father, Nizhnyi Novgorod, head of chemistry department, the Red Army, taken prisoner by Denikin, biography of a Russian youth, father a merchant, was an inventor, dealt with Moscow restaurants. Talked to him throughout the journey. We are going to Milatyn, on the way there—plums. In Stary Milatyn the church, the Catholic priest's apartment, the priest has a luxurious apartment, it's unforgettable, he keeps shaking my hand every other minute, is on his way to bury a dead Pole, but sits down a bit, asks whether our commander is a good man, a typically Jesuitical face, clean-shaven, shifty gray eyes, says how good it all is, a tearful Polish woman, his niece, begs us to give her back her heifer, tears and a coquettish smile, all very Polish. Mustn't forget the apartment, bric-a-brac, pleasant darkness, Jesuitical, Catholic culture, clean women and the extraordinarily fragrant, overanxious priest with a monastery across the way. I want to stay on. We wait for a decision—are we to stay in old or new Milatyn. Night. A panic. Somebody's baggage train, the Poles have broken through somewhere, all hell let loose on the road, wagons three abreast, I am in the Milatyn school, two handsome old maids, alarming how much they remind me of the Shapiro sisters from Nikolayev, two quiet, educated Galician women, patriots, their own culture, their bedroom, probably hair curlers, in this rumbling, roaring, embattled Milatyn, beyond these walls wagon trains, cannon, our fatherly commanders telling their tales of heroism, orange-colored dust, clouds of dust, the monastery is swathed in dust. The sisters offer me cigarettes, they breathe in my words about how splendid everything is going to be, it's balm to them, they blossom, and suddenly we're discussing cultural matters, like intellectuals.

A knock at the door. The commander wants me. A scare. We ride to New Milatyn. *N. Milatyn.* With the military commissar in the almshouse, a roofed yard, sheds, night, cellars, the priest's servant girl, gloomy, dirty, myriads of flies, indescribable fatigue, the fatigue of the front.

Daybreak, we ride out, we have to breach the railroad (all this is happening on 17 Aug.), the Brody-Lvov line.

My first battle, I saw the attack, they assemble in the bushes, the brigade commanders ride up to Apanasenko—cautious Kniga, the crafty one, rides over, showers him with words, they point at the hills—just before that wood there, up above that hollow, they've spotted the enemy, the regiments rush in to attack, swords flashing in the sun, pale commanders, Apanasenko's sturdy legs, hurrah.

What's happened? The open field, dust, the staff on level ground, Apanasenko swearing furiously, the brigade commander—annihilate the bastards, effing bandits.

Mood before the battle, hunger, heat, galloping into the attack, the nurses.

A roar of hurrahs, the Poles are crushed, we ride onto the battlefield, a little Pole with polished fingernails rubs his pink head, sparse hair, answers evasively, wriggles, hems and haws, well, yes, Sheko, roused, pale, answer the question, who are you, I'm a—hums and haws—sort of ensign, we ride a little way off, he is led away, there's a lad with a nice face behind him, he loads his gun. I shout out—"Yakov Vasilyevich!" "Yakov Vasilyevich!" He pretends not to hear, rides on, a shot, the little Pole in his underpants falls on his face and twitches. Life is loathsome, murderers, it's unbearable, baseness and crime.

The prisoners are rounded up, made to undress, a strange scene, they undress terribly quickly, shaking their heads, all this out in the sun, a bit embarrassing, all the commanders are there, embarrassing, but who cares, shut your eyes to it. I won't forget that "sort of" ensign, treacherously murdered.

Ahead—horrible things. We crossed the railroad at Zadworze. The Poles are fighting their way along the line toward Lvov. An attack in the evening near a farm. A bloody battle. The military commissar and I ride along the line begging the men not to massacre prisoners. Apanasenko washes his hands of it. Sheko's tongue ran away with him—the massacres have played a terrible role. I couldn't look at their faces, they bayoneted some, shot others, bodies covered by corpses, they strip one man while they're shooting another, groans, screams, death rattles, the attack was carried out by our squadron, Apanasenko remained aloof, the squadron dressed itself up as expected, Matusevich's horse was killed under him, he runs around with a terrible, dirty face looking for a horse.

It's hell. Our way of bringing freedom—horrible. They search the farm, drag people out, Apanasenko—don't waste cartridges, stick them. That's what Apanasenko always says—stick the nurse, stick the Poles.

We spend the night in Zadworze, poor quarters, I'm with Sheko, good food, uninterrupted fighting, I'm living a soldier's life, completely worn out, we are stationed in the forest, nothing to eat all day, Sheko's carriage arrives, brings something, I'm often at the observation point, the batteries at work, the forest fringes, hollows, machine guns mowing people down, the Poles are defending themselves mainly with aeroplanes, they're becoming a menace, describe an air attack, the distant, deceptively slow rattle of a machine gun, panic in the wagon trains, nerve-racking, they glide overhead incessantly, we hide from them. A new use of aviation, I think of Mosher, Captain Fauntleroy is in Lvov, our peregrination from one brigade to another, Kniga—only flanking movements, Kolesnikov—frontal attack, Sheko and I ride out to reconnoiter, unbroken forest, deadly danger, on the hills, bullets hum around us before the attack, Sukhorukov with a pitiful look on his face and a saber, I tag along behind the staff, we are waiting for reports, but they keep going, taking roundabout ways.

The fighting for Barszczowice. After a day of ups and downs Polish columns are breaking through to Lvov toward evening. When Apanasenko saw what had happened he went mad, started shaking, the brigades are throwing everything into it, although they're dealing with a retreating enemy, the brigades are strung out in endless lines, three cavalry brigades are thrown in, Apanasenko is triumphant, snorts, sends in a new man, Litovchenko, to command the 3rd Brigade, in place of the wounded Kolesnikov, look, there they are, go in and destroy them, they're on the run, he corrects the artillery fire, interferes with the orders of battery commanders, feverish expectation, they hoped to repeat what happened at Zadworze, but it didn't work out. Marsh on one side, withering fire on the other. A move on Ostrów, the 6th Cavalry Division must take Lvov from the southeast.

Colossal losses among command personnel: Korochaev badly wounded, his deputy killed—the Jew killed, commander of 34th Regiment wounded, all the commissars of 31st Regiment out of action, all the brigade chiefs of staff wounded, Budyonny's commanders head the list.

The wounded crawl onto tachankas. And this is what we call taking Lvov, reports to the army commander are written in the grass, the brigades gallop on, orders in the night, the forest again, bullets humming past, artillery fire drives us from place to place, nagging fear of airplanes, hurry up, it's about to explode, a nasty taste in the mouth, and you run. No fodder for the horses.

I understand now what a horse means to a Cossack or a cavalryman.

Unhorsed riders on hot, dusty roads, carrying their saddles, sleeping like the dead on other people's wagons, rotting horses everywhere, the talk is all about horses, the custom of exchanging them, wild gallops, horses are martyrs, horses are long-suffering, they are epic figures, I'm imbued with this feeling myself, with every day's ride I suffer for my horse.

Apanasenko and his retinue go to see Budyonny. Budyonny and Voroshilov are in a farmhouse sitting at a table. Apanasenko reports, standing at attention. Failure of the special regiment—they planned a surprise attack on Lvov, took the field, but the special regiment's sentries were asleep, as usual, were stood down, the Poles hauled up a machine gun to within a hundred paces, lured the horses out and wounded half the regiment.

Savior's Day—19 August—in Barszczowice, a half-dead but still breathing village, peace, water meadows, lots of geese (we dealt with them later, Sidorenko and Egor beheading geese on a plank with their swords), we eat stewed goose, that same day, they make the village beautiful, white geese on green meadows, the villagers observe the holiday but look feeble, spectral, scarcely able to crawl out of their hovels, silent, strange, bewildered, completely crushed.

There's something about the holiday that's subdued and oppressive.

The Uniate priest at Barszczowice. A ruined, desecrated garden, Budyonny's staff had been here, a beehive smashed and burned, that's a horrifying, barbaric custom, I remember the shattered frames, thousands of bees, buzzing and hurtling round the ruined hive in anxious swarms.

The priest explains to me the difference between the Uniate faith and Orthodoxy. Says Szeptycki is a great man, wears a canvas cassock. Rather fat, with a puffy dark face, cheeks clean-shaven, bright little eyes with a sty.

Advancing on Lvov. Batteries are getting nearer and nearer. Not very successful battle near Ostrów, the Poles withdraw nonetheless. Information on Lvov's defenses—professors, women, adolescents. Apanasenko will massacre them, he hates the intelligentsia, and it goes deep, he wants a state of peasants and Cossacks, aristocratic in its own peculiar way.

A week of battle is over—on 21 August our units are 4 versts short of Lvov.

An order—the whole Cavalry Army is now at the disposal of Western Command. We are being moved north—toward Lublin. An attack is being mounted there. They're pulling out the army, now standing 4 versts outside the city, which we've been trying to take for so long. We're to be replaced by the 14th Army. What is this—madness or the impossibility of taking the city with cavalry? The 45-verst transit from Barszczowice to Adamy I shall remember all my life. I myself on my little skewbald horse, Sheko in a carriage, heat and dust, dust from the Apocalypse, suffocating clouds of it, endless wagon trains, all the brigades on the move, clouds of dust from which there is no escape, you choke horribly, all around shouting, movement, I ride out over the fields with the squadron, we lose Sheko, the most terrible part of it begins, riding my laggard horse, riding endlessly, always at a trot, I'm thoroughly drained, the squadron tries to overtake the wagons, we try to overtake them, I'm afraid of being left behind, my horse drifts along like thistledown, by inertia, all the brigades are on the move, all the artillery, they've each left one regiment behind to cover them, these are supposed to join up with the division when darkness sets in. We ride through dead, silent Busk in the night. What is so special about Galician towns? That mixture of the dirty and sluggish East (Byzantium and the Jews) with the beery German West. 15 kilometers from Busk. I'm not going to be able to stand it. I exchange horses. Turns out there's no cover on the saddle. Riding is torture. I change my position from one minute to the next. Stop for a rest in Kozłów. Dark hut, bread and milk. Some peasant, a mild, hospitable person, had been a prisoner of war in Odessa, I lie on the bench, mustn't go to sleep, am wearing somebody else's tunic, horses in the dark, stuffy in the hut, children on the floor. We arrive in Adamy at 4 a.m. Sheko is asleep. I hitch the horse somewhere, there's hay, I lie down to sleep.

21 August 1920. Adamy

Frightened Ruthenians. Sunshine. It's good. I'm sick. Rest. I spend all day in the barn, sleep, feel better in the evening, but my head is pounding, aching. I'm lodging with Sheko. The div. chief of staff's lackey, Egor. We eat well. How we get food. Vorobyov has taken over the 2nd Squadron. The soldiers are pleased. In Poland, where we're going, we won't have to stand on ceremony, here with these Galicians, who are not to blame for anything, we had to be more careful. I'm resting up, can't sit in the saddle.

Conversation with Maksimov, divisional artillery commander, our army is out to line its pockets, this isn't a revolution, it's a rebellion of Cossack wild men.

It is simply a means to an end, one the Party does not disdain.

Two Odessans—Manuilov and Boguslavsky, military commissar of the air squadron, Paris, London, a handsome Jew, a braggart, article in a European newspaper, aide to the div. chief of staff, Jews in the Cavalry Army. I tell them what's what. Dressed in a smart tunic, the excesses of the Odessa bourgeoisie, distressing news from

Odessa. They're being suffocated. What's happening to my father? Have they really taken everything away from him? I must think about things at home.

I'm becoming a scrounger.

Apanasenko has written a letter to Polish officers. Bandits, stop the war, surrender, or we'll cut you all to bits, my fine Polish gentlemen. Apanasenko's letter to the Don, to Stavropol, they're making things difficult for our soldiers back there—sons of the Revolution, we are heroes, we are fearless, we march on.

Describe the squadron at rest, the squealing of pigs, hens stolen, agents, fanfares out on the square. They wash their laundry, thresh oats, gallop around with sheaves, the horses, ears twitching, munch oats. The horse is everything. Their names—Stepan, Misha, Little Brother, Old Girl. The horse is his savior—the Cossack is aware of that every minute of the day, but can nonetheless thrash it inhumanly. Nobody is looking after my horse. Nobody is bothering much.

22 August 1920. Adamy

Manuilov—adjutant to the chief of staff—has a bellyache. Of course. He has served with Muravyov, in the Cheka, something to do with the military-prosecution service, a bourgeois, women, Paris, aviation, some affair of honor—and he's a communist. Boguslavsky, the secretary, scared, says nothing and eats.

A peaceful day. Move farther north.

I am lodging with Sheko. Can't do anything. Tired, shattered. I sleep and eat. How we eat. The system. Army stores and foraging parties give us nothing. Red troops arrive in a village, ransack the place, cook, stoves crackling all night, the householders' daughters have a hard time, pigs squealing, they present their receipts to the military commissar. These poor Galicians.

It's a whole epic, the way we eat. We eat well—pigs, hens, geese. Those who refrain are "looters," "milksops."

23–24 August 1920. Witków

Rode on to Witków in a cart. The system of using local carriers, unfortunate local people, worked to death for two or three weeks, then they're let off, given a pass, but another lot of soldiers take them over, and drive them as hard as before. A rare occurrence—while we were there a youngster came home from the wagon train. Night. His mother's joy.

We're moving into the Krasnystaw-Lublin district. Have overtaken the army, which was 4 versts from Lvov. The cavalry couldn't take the place.

The road to Witków. Sunshine. Galician roads, interminable baggage trains, remount horses, devastated Galicia, the Jews in the towns, somewhere an undamaged farm, Czech, I dare say, raid on unripe apples, on the beehives.

More about the beehives another time.

Along the way, on the cart, my thoughts, grief for the future of the Revolution.

The town is an unusual one, rebuilt to a master plan after its destruction, little white houses, high wooden roofs, the sadness of it all.

I am living with the adjutants to the div. chief of staff. Manuilov has no understanding of staff work at all, trials and tribulations with the horses, no one will give us any, we have to ride on villagers' carts, Boguslavsky wears lilac-colored undershorts, is a great success with the girls in Odessa.

The soldiers ask for a show. They're fed "The Orderly Pulls a Fast One."

The div. chief of staff's night—where's the 33rd Regiment, where's the 2nd Brigade got to, telephone, orders from army HQ to commanders of 1st, 2nd, 3rd Brigades!

Duty dispatch riders. Composition of the squadrons, squadron commanders—Matusevich and the former commander Vorobyov, an invariably good-humored and, I imagine, stupid man.

The div. chief of staff's night—you're wanted by the div. commander.

25 August 1920. Sokal

A city at last. We go through a town called Tartaków, Jews, ruins, Jewish-type cleanliness, race, little shops.

I'm still ill, cannot get over the battles around Lvov. How stale the air is in these towns. The infantry has been in Sokal, but the city is untouched. The div. chief of staff is lodging with some Jews. Books, I've seen some books. I am lodging with a Galician woman, a rich one at that, we eat well, chicken in sour cream.

I go to the center of town on horseback, it's clean, handsome buildings, everything messed up by war, but vestiges of cleanliness and a character of its own.

The Revolutionary Committee. Requisitions and confiscations. Curious: they don't touch the peasantry at all. All the land is at its disposal. The peasantry are not involved.

Declarations of the Revolutionary Committee.

My landlord's son is a Zionist and ein angesprochener Nationalist. Normal Jewish life. They feel the pull of Vienna, Berlin, the nephew, a very young man, studies philosophy and wants to go to university. We eat butter and chocolate. Candy.

Friction between Manuilov and the div. chief of staff. Sheko tells him to go to . . .

"I have my pride," they won't let him get any sleep, no horse, that's the Cavalry Army for you, never get any rest here. The books—polnische, juden.

In the evening—div. commander in a new tunic, well-fed, particolored breeches, red-faced and obtuse, amusing himself—music in the night, the rain dispersed us. It's raining, excruciating Galician rain, it pours and pours, endlessly, hopelessly.

What are our soldiers doing in the town? Dark rumors.

Boguslavsky has betrayed Manuilov. Boguslavsky is a slave.

26 August 1920. Sokal

Look around the town with the young Zionist. Synagogues—the Hasidic one, a deeply moving sight, 300 years ago, pale, handsome boys with peyes, another synagogue 200 years old, the same little figures in gaberdines, swaying, waving their arms, wailing. This is the orthodox party—they support the Rabbi of Bełz, the famous Bełz rabbi who has run away to Vienna. The moderates support the Husiatyn rabbi. Their synagogue. The beauty of the altar, made by some local craftsman, the splendor of the greenish chandeliers, the worm-eaten tables, the Bełz party's synagogue is a vision of times long gone. The Jews ask me to use my influence to save them from ruin, they are being robbed of food and goods.

The Yids hide everything. The cobbler, the Sokal cobbler, is a proletarian. His apprentice's appearance—the redheaded Hasid is a cobbler.

The cobbler had looked forward to Soviet rule—and what he sees are Jew-baiters and looters, and that he won't be earning anything, he is dismayed and looks at us mistrustfully. Confusion over money. Strictly speaking we pay nothing, 15–20 rubles. The Jewish quarter. Indescribable poverty, filth, the seclusion of the ghetto.

Little shops, all open, whiting and pitch, soldiers rummaging, cursing the Yids, sauntering around aimlessly, walking into people's living quarters, crawling under counters, greedy eyes, shaky hands, a peculiar sort of army.

Organized looting of a stationer's shop, the proprietor in tears, they tear up everything, make demands, the daughter shows Western European self-possession, but pitiful and red-faced, hands things over, is given what passes for money, with her shopkeeper's politeness tries to make it look as if everything were normal, except that there are too many customers. The proprietor's wife in despair, can't make sense of it all.

When night comes the whole town will be looted—everybody knows it.

In the evening, music—the div. commander enjoys himself. This morning he wrote to the Don and to Stavropol. The army at the front cannot tolerate the disgraceful goings-on in the rear. Look who's talking!

The div. commander's lackeys parade his stately horses with brasses on their breasts and ribbons in their tails.

The military commissar and the nurse. He's a real Russian—a sly peasant, rough, sometimes insolent and muddleheaded. He thinks highly of the nurse, sounds me out, questions me about her, he's in love.

The nurse goes to say good-bye to the div. commander, this after all that's happened. Everybody's slept with her. That lout Suslov is in the adjoining room—says the div. commander is busy cleaning his revolver.

I get boots and some linen. Sukhorukov got some, divided it up himself, he's the arch-lackey, must describe him.

Conversation with the nephew who wants to go to university.

Sokal is brokers and artisans, communism, they tell me, isn't likely to catch on here.

What badly shaken, tormented people.

Ill-fated Galicia, ill-fated Jews.

My landlord has 8 pigeons.

Manuilov at daggers drawn with Sheko, he has many sins in his past. A Kiev adventurer. Came to us demoted, was chief of staff in the 3rd Brigade.

Lepin. A dark, passionate soul.

The nurse—26 men and a girl.

27 August 1920

Battles at Źniatyn, Dłuźniów. We're moving northwest. Half the day with the wagon train. Route lies through Łaszczów, Komarów. We left Sokal in the morning. A normal day—with the squadrons, with the div. commander, wandering through woods and clearings, the brigade commanders ride over to us, hot sun, haven't dismounted for 5 hours, the brigades ride past. Panic in the wagon train. I leave the wagons on the outskirts of the forest, ride over to the div. commander. Squadrons up on a hill. Reports to the army commander, artillery fire, no aeroplanes, we ride from place to place, a normal day. Dead tired by nightfall. To Wasyłów for the night. We have not reached our destination, Łaszczów.

The 11th Division is in Wasyłów or somewhere near, chaos. Bakhturov—a tiny division, he has lost some of his luster, the 4th Division is fighting successfully.

28 August 1920. Komarów

I rode out of Wasyłów ten minutes behind the squadrons. With three other riders. Hillocks, clearings, ruined farms, somewhere amid the greenery are red columns, plums. Gunfire somewhere, we don't know where the enemy is, nobody in sight, machine guns chattering quite near and from different directions, my heart sinks, it's the same every day, lone riders looking for their HQ, carrying reports. Toward noon I found the squadron in a devastated village (all the inhabitants were hiding in their cellars), under trees laden with plums. I ride on with the squadron. We enter Komarów with the div. commander, wearing his red hood. Magnificent unfinished red church. Before we entered Komarów, after the firing— was riding by myself—silence, warmth, a fine day, a strange, translucent serenity, my soul gently aching, alone, nobody to get on my nerves, fields, woods, undulating valleys, shady roads.

We halt opposite the church.

Voroshilov and Budyonny arrive. Voroshilov gives the div. commander a dressing-down, with everybody listening, "lack of energy," gets heated, a hot-tempered man, gingers up the whole army, rides back and forth shouting, Budyonny says nothing, smiles, white teeth. Apanasenko tries to defend himself, "let's go inside," "why," Voroshilov shouts, "we're letting the enemy get away, losing contact, without contact we can't strike."

Apanasenko not up to it?

The pharmacist, offering me a room. Rumor of atrocities. I walk into town. Indescribable terror and despair.

They tell me all about it. Privately, indoors, they're afraid the Poles may come back. Captain Yakovlev's Cossacks were here yesterday. A pogrom. The family of David Zys, in people's homes, a naked, barely breathing prophet of an old man, an old woman butchered, a child with fingers chopped off, many people still breathing, stench of blood, everything turned upside down, chaos, a mother sitting over her sabered son, an old woman lying twisted up like a pretzel, four people in one hovel, filth, blood under a black beard, just lying there in their blood. The Jews on the square, an agonized Jew showing it all to me, a tall Jew takes over from him. The rabbi hid, his whole house was taken apart, he waited till evening to creep out of his hole. 15 people killed, the Hasid Itska Galer, aged 70, David Zys, the synagogue caretaker, 45, his wife, his daughter, aged 15, David Trost and his wife—the ritual slaughterer.

At the home of a rape victim.

In the evening—with my hosts, like a prison, Saturday evening, they wouldn't cook till Sabbath was over.

I go looking for the nurses. Suslov laughs. A Jewish woman doctor.

We are in a strange, old-world house, once they had everything—butter, milk.

At night, a walk around the town.

Moonlight, their life at night, behind closed doors. Wailing beyond those walls. They'll clean it all up. The fear and horror of the inhabitants. The worst of it is—our men nonchalantly walk around looting wherever possible, stripping mangled corpses.

The hatred is the same, the Cossacks just the same, the cruelty the same, it's nonsense to think one army is different from another. The life of these little towns. There's no salvation. Everyone destroys them—the Poles gave them no refuge. The girls and women, all of them, can scarcely walk. In the evening—a talkative Jew with a little beard, used to keep a shop, daughter threw herself out of a second-story window to escape a Cossack, broke her arms, one of many.

What a mighty and marvelous life of a nation existed here. The fate of Jewry. At our place in the evening, supper, tea, I sit and drink in the words of the Jew with the little beard, wistfully asking me whether it will be possible to trade.

An oppressive, uneasy night.

29 August 1920. Komarów, Łabunie, Pniowek

Withdrawal from Komarów. Our men were looting last night, tossed out the Torah scrolls in the synagogue and took the velvet covers for saddlecloths. The military commissar's dispatch rider examines phylacteries, wants to take the straps. The Jews smile ingratiatingly. That's religion.

They all look greedily at what they may have missed, rummage among bones and ruins. That's what they're here for, to earn.

My horse is lame, I take the div. chief of staff's horse, I want to exchange mine, I'm too soft, talk to the village headman, nothing comes of it.

Łabunie. A vodka distillery. 8,000 vedros of spirits. Guarded. Rain, penetrating, incessant. Autumn, everything says it's autumn. The bailiff's Polish family. Horses under an awning, Red Army men drinking in spite of the ban. Łabunie is a terrible menace to the army.

Everything hidden, nothing out of the ordinary. People silent, nothing meets the eye. Oh, the Russian. Everything breathes secrecy and menace. Sidorenko has calmed down.

Operation to take Zamość. We are 10 versts from Zamość. When we get there I'll ask about R. Yu.

The operation, as usual, is uncomplicated, make a flanking movement to the west and north of the town, and take it. Alarming news from western front. The Poles have taken Białystok.

We ride on. The Kułaczkowski estate at Łabunka plundered. White pillars. Enchanting though seigneurial establishment. Unimaginable destruction. The real Poland—bailiffs, old women, tow-haired children, rich semi-European villages, village headmen and district headmen, all Catholics, beautiful women. Our men steal oats on the estate. Horses in the drawing room, black horses. Well, we've got to keep the rain off them. Priceless books in a chest, they were in too much of a hurry to take them along—a copy of the constitution approved by the Sejm at the beginning of the 18th century, old folio volumes from the reign of Nicholas I, Polish Code of Laws, precious bindings, 16th-century Polish manuscripts, monkish chronicles, old French novels.

Upstairs no destruction, just a search, all the chairs, walls, sofas ripped open, floorboards pulled up, no, they weren't wrecking the place, just searching. Fine cut glass, bedroom, oak beds, lady's dressing table, French novels on little tables, many French and Polish books on child care, intimate women's accoutrements all smashed, some butter left in a butter dish, newlyweds?

A settled way of life, gymnastic equipment, good books, tables, jars containing medicines, everything sacrilegiously mutilated. An unbearable feeling, I want to run away from these vandals, but they walk around, searching, describe their gait, their faces, their hats, their foul language, as they drag sheaves of oats through the clinging mud.

We are approaching Zamość. A terrible day. The rain is the victor, it doesn't let up for a minute. The horses can hardly pull their hooves out of the mud. Describe this intolerable rain. We struggle on far into the night. We are soaked through, weary, Apanasenko's red cap. We make a detour around Zamość, our units are 3–4 versts away from it. The armored trains won't let us get any nearer, keep us under fire. We sit in the fields, wait for reports, muddy streams swirl round us. Brigade Commander Kniga in a shack, report. Our Father and commander. We can't do anything about the armored trains. It turns out that we didn't know there was a railroad here, it isn't marked on the map, a mix-up, so much for our reconnaissance.

We hang around, keep waiting for Zamość to be taken. Damn it all. The Poles are fighting better all the time. Men and horses shivering. We spend the night in Pniowek. A handsome Polish peasant family. The difference between Russians and Poles is striking. The Poles live a cleaner, gayer life, play with their children, beautiful icons, beautiful women.

30 August 1920

Morning—we leave Pniowek. The drive on Zamość continues. The weather is as horrible as ever, rain, slush, roads impassable, practically no sleep, on the floor, on straw, in our boots—must be prepared.

More hanging around. Sheko and I ride over to the 3rd Brigade. He goes to attack Zawady station, revolver in hand. Lepin and I stay in the forest. Lepin in agonies. The battle at the station. Sheko has a do-or-die look. Describe "rapid fire." We've taken the station. We ride up to the railroad track. Ten prisoners, we are too late to save one of them. Revolver wound? An officer. Bleeding from the mouth. Thick red blood, clotted, inundates his face, his face is horrible, red, covered with a thick coating of blood. The prisoners are all undressed. The squadron commander has a pair of breeches slung over his saddle. Sheko makes him give them back. They try to make the prisoners dress, they won't. Officer's service cap. "There were nine of them." Filthy language all around them. The men want to kill them. Bald-headed, lame Jew in his undershorts, couldn't keep up with his horse, terrible face, probably an officer, gets on everybody's nerves, can't walk, all of them in a state of animal terror, pitiful, unfortunate people, Polish proletarians, another Pole, stately, composed, with side whiskers, wearing a knitted sweater, dignified demeanor, they keep asking whether he's an officer. The men want to butcher them. A storm gathers over the Jew. A furious Putilov worker says we ought to kill the lot of them, the bastards, the Jew hops along behind us, we drag prisoners with us all the time, then hand them over to the authority of escort troops. What will become of them? The Putilov worker's fury, foaming at the mouth, sword out, I'll cut the bastards up, and I won't have to answer for it.

We ride over to the div. commander, he's with the 1st and 2nd

Brigades. We are in sight of Zamość all the time, can see its chimneys, houses, we are trying to take it from all sides. A night attack is in preparation. We are 3 versts from Zamość, awaiting its capture, we'll spend the night there. Open field, night, rain, piercing cold, we lie on the wet ground, nothing to give the horses, dark, messages arrive. 1st and 3rd Brigades will carry out the attack. Kniga and Levda, commander of 3rd Brigade, a semi-literate Ukrainian, arrive as usual. Weariness, apathy, unconquerable longing to sleep, almost despair. A cordon advances in the dark, a whole brigade on foot. There's a cannon alongside us. An hour later the infantry goes in. Our cannon fires uninterruptedly, a soft popping sound, the night is lit up, the Poles are letting off rockets, frenzied shooting from rifles and machine guns, hellish, we wait, it's after 2 a.m. The fighting is petering out. We have gotten nowhere. We get nowhere more and more frequently. What does it mean? Is the army folding up?

We ride 10 versts or so to Sitaniec for the night. The rain is getting heavier. Indescribable tiredness. My one dream—a billet. My dream comes true. A bewildered old Pole and his wife. The soldiers, of course, take everything he has. Extremely frightened, they've all been sitting in cellars. Lots of milk, butter, noodles, bliss. I keep ferreting out more food. Nice old woman at the limit of her endurance. Delicious rendered butter. Suddenly shots, bullets whistle around the stables, around the horses' legs. We break it up fast. Despair. We ride to the other end of the village. Three hours' sleep, broken by reports, debriefings, alerts.

31 August 1920. Cześniki

Conference with brigade commanders. Farmhouse. A shady clearing in the wood. Total destruction. Not even clothes left. We pinch every last speck of oats. The orchard, apiary, destruction of the hives, terrible, bees buzzing despairingly, the men blow up the hives with gunpowder, muffle themselves up in their greatcoats and attack the hives, a wild orgy, they tear the frames out with their sabers, honey drips onto the ground, the bees sting them, they smoke them out with tarred rags, lighted rags. Cherkashin. In the apiary chaos, total destruction, smoking ruins.

I'm writing in the orchard, a grassy glade, flowers, I feel sick about it all.

Orders from army HQ to leave Zamość, go to the rescue of the 14th Division, which is under pressure from the direction of Komarów. The Poles have reoccupied the town. Poor Komarów. Ride along the flank. The enemy cavalry is right before us—an open field, nobody we'd sooner carve up than Captain Yakovlev and his Cossacks. An attack is imminent. The brigades are massing in the forest—some two versts from Cześniki.

Voroshilov and Budyonny are with us the whole time. Voroshilov is short, graying, wears red breeches with silver stripes, always hurrying people up, tense, keeps nagging Apanasenko about why the 2nd Brigade isn't here yet. We're waiting for the 2nd Brigade to join us. Time drags excruciatingly. Don't hurry me, Comrade Voroshilov. Voroshilov—it's all over, shot to hell.

Budyonny says nothing, smiles occasionally, showing his dazzling white teeth. A brigade must be sent in first, then a regiment. Voroshilov can't wait, he sends in everyone he's got. The regiment parades for Voroshilov and Budyonny. Voroshilov pulls out an enormous revolver—show the Polish gents no mercy, his harangue is received with approval. The regiment rushes out in disorder, hurrah, let them have it, one gallops, another keeps a tight rein, a third is trotting, the horses won't go, mess tins and carpet cloth. Our squadron joins the attack. We gallop about 4 versts. They're waiting for us on the hill, drawn up in columns. Amazing—not one man budges. Steadfastness, discipline. An officer with a black beard. I am being fired at. My sensations. Flight. The military commissars try to turn the fleeing men. Nothing helps. Fortunately the enemy doesn't pursue, otherwise there would be a catastrophe. Our side try to reassemble the brigade for a second attack, but without success. Manuilov is threatened with revolvers. Our only heroes are heroines—the nurses.

We ride back. Sheko's horse is wounded, he himself is shell-shocked, his frightening, stony face. He can't make out what's happening, he weeps, we lead his horse. It's bleeding heavily.

The nurse talking—some nurses are always looking for sympathy, they say we're there to help the fighting man, we share all his hardships, I'd shoot that sort, she says, only what with, with my dick, maybe, only I haven't got one.

The command is despondent, menacing signs that the army is disintegrating. Cheerful, featherbrained Vorobyov, recounts his feats, galloped right up to them, fired four times point-blank. Apanasenko suddenly turns around, you ruined the attack, you rotter.

Apanasenko in a black mood, Sheko pathetic.

Some are saying the army isn't what it was, time it was given a rest. What next. We spend the night at Cześniki—chilled to the bone, weary, silent, mud impassable, sucks you in, autumn, roads rutted, misery. Dismal prospects ahead.

1 September 1920. Terebin

We leave Cześniki in the night. We had halted there for two hours or so. Night, cold, on horseback. We tremble. Order from army HQ—withdraw, we're surrounded, we've lost contact with the 12th Army, no contact with anybody. Sheko weeps, his head trembles, his face is that of a hurt child, pathetic, shattered. People are despicable. Vinokurov wouldn't let him read the army order—he's suspended. Apanasenko reluctantly gives him a carriage—what do they think I am, a cabby?

Endless discussion of yesterday's attack, bunch of lies, sincere regrets, the men say nothing. Vorobyov, that idiot, booms away. The div. commander shuts him up.

Beginning of the end for the 1st Cavalry Army. Talk of a retreat.

Sheko—a man in misfortune.

Manuilov has a temperature of 40, fever, everybody hates him, he persecutes Sheko, why? He doesn't know how to behave. The sly, insinuating, out-for-himself dispatch rider Borisov, nobody is sorry for him—that's what's so horrible. A Jew?

The army is saved by the 4th Division. By the "traitor" Timoshenko.

We reach Terebin, a half-ruined village, cold. Autumn, I sleep in a barn in the daytime, with Sheko at night.

Conversation with Arzam Slyagit. Riding together. We talk about Tiflis, fruit, sunshine. I think about Odessa, my heart breaks.

We have Sheko's bleeding horse in tow.

2 September 1920. Terebin—Metelin

Miserable villages. Jerry-built hovels. Half-naked inhabitants. We ruin it completely. The div. commander with the troops. Army order—hold back the enemy, who is making for the Bug, attack along a line between Wakijów and Hostyne. We exchange blows, but can't hold on to our gains. Talk about the decline of the army's fighting fitness more and more persistent. Desertions from the army. Countless reports of men on leave, men off sick.

The div. commander's worst affliction is the lack of real commanders, they're all promoted from the ranks, Apanasenko hates the "democrats," says they understand nothing, there's nobody to lead a regiment into an attack.

Squadron commanders are commanding regiments.

Days of apathy, Sheko is recovering, depressed. It's a grim life, in the atmosphere of an army that's cracking up.

3, 4, 5 September 1920. Malice

We have moved on to Malice.

Our new divisional adjutant is Orlov. A Gogolian figure. Pathological bullshitter, never stops talking, Jewish features, the most striking thing, if you give it any thought, is the horrifying frivolity of his talk, chatter, bullshit. He is in pain (limps), a partisan, formerly one of Makhno's band, went to secondary school, has commanded a regiment. This frivolity frightens me. Is there anything more to him?

Manuilov has finally taken off, though not without a scene, he was threatened with arrest, what muddleheadedness on Sheko's part, he was sent first to the 1st Brigade, the idiocy of it, army HQ has transferred him to the air force. Amen.

I am living with Sheko. He is obtuse, good-natured if you keep on the right side of him, talentless, not strong-willed. I lick his boots—and I eat. The languid semi-Odessan Boguslavsky, who dreams all the time about the "little girls" in Odessa, will if pushed ride to collect an army order at night. Boguslavsky on a Cossack saddle.

1st Platoon of the 1st Squadron. Kuban Cossacks. They sing songs. Well-behaved. They smile. Don't make too much noise.

Levda reported sick. Crafty Ukrainian. "Got rheumatism, not well enough to work." Three reports from brigades, concerted—if they're not pulled out for a rest the division is doomed, no fighting spirit, the horses run off their feet, men dispirited. The 3rd Brigade has been out in the open for two days, cold, rain.

A sad country, impassable mud, men missing, they hide their horses in the forest, quietly weeping women.

Report from Kniga—"Being unable to cope without a command group . . ."

All the horses are in the woods, the soldiers are exchanging them—a science, and a sport.

Barsukov is cracking up. Wants to go to school.

Battles under way. Our side trying to advance in the direction of Wakijów-Honiatyczki. And getting nowhere. We're strangely impotent.

The Pole is slowly but surely squeezing us out. The div. commander isn't up to it, neither initiative, nor the necessary doggedness. His festering ambition, womanizing, gluttony—and, probably, feverish activity should it be needed.

This way of life.

Kniga writes that the previous high spirits are no more, the soldiers walk around apathetically.

Depressing weather all the time, roads churned up, terrible Russian country mud, you can't pull your boots out of it, no sun, rain, overcast, an accursed country.

I'm sick, quinsy, fever, can hardly move, terrible nights in suffocating, smoke-filled cottages, on straw, my body is covered with scratches and bites, itching, bleeding, nothing I can do.

Military operations continue sluggishly, a period of equilibrium with the balance beginning to tip toward the Poles.

The command is passive or rather nonexistent.

I run over to the nurse for dressings, have to go through back gardens, tenacious mud. The nurse lives with a platoon. A heroine, even if she does sleep around. A cottage, men smoking, swearing, changing their foot cloths, the soldier's life, one other person there—the nurse. Anybody too fussy to drink out of the single cup is thrown out.

The enemy is on the offensive. We took Lotów, are surrendering it, he's squeezing us out, not a single attack of ours succeeds, we send the baggage train on, I ride to Terebin on Barsukov's cart, the rest is rain, slush, misery, we cross the Bug, Budyatichi. So it has been decided to surrender the Bug line.

6 September 1920. Budyatichi

Budyatichi occupied by 44th Division. Clashes. They were taken aback by the wild horde rushing in on them. Orlov—hand it over and get out.

A nurse, a proud, dim-witted, beautiful nurse in tears, a doctor outraged by yells of "Smash the Yids, save Russia!" They are stunned, the quartermaster has been thrashed with a whip, the contents of the clinic tossed out, pigs requisitioned and dragged off without receipt—and they had things in order, all sorts of plenipotentiaries visit Sheko with complaints. That's Budyonny's warriors for you.

The proud nurse, we've never seen one like her—in low white shoes and white stockings, a plump, shapely leg, they have organization, respect for human dignity, their work is quick and thorough.

We are lodging with Jews.

My thoughts of home are more and more insistent. I cannot see where it will end.

7 September 1920. Budyatichi

We're occupying two rooms. The kitchen is full of Jews. There are refugees from Kryłow, a pathetic little bunch of people with the faces of prophets. They sleep in a heap. They spend the whole day cooking and baking, the Jewish woman works like a galley slave, sewing, washing. They pray there on the spot. Children, young women. The louts and lackeys gorge continuously, drink vodka, guffaw, get fat, choke with lust for a woman.

We eat every two hours.

Our unit has been pulled back over the Bug, a new phase of the operation.

For two weeks now they've been talking more and more emphatically about the need to pull the army out for a rest. Let's rest—that's our battle cry!

An inspection team shows up—entertained by the div. commander—they're always eating, his stories of Stavropol, Suslov is getting fat, he's well provided, the lout.

Terrible tactlessness—Sheko, Suslov, Sukhorukov have been recommended for the Order of the Red Banner.

The enemy is trying to cross to our side of the Bug, the 14th Division, dismounted, fought him off.

I issue certificates.

Have gone deaf in one ear. Result of my chill? My body is scratched all over, abrasions everywhere, I'm losing strength. Autumn, rain, dreariness, dreadful mud.

8 September 1920. Vladimir-Volynsk

This morning, on a civilian cart to administrative HQ. Have to testify, some muddle over money. Revolting behavior of people semidetached from the front—Gusev, Nalyotov, money with the Revolutionary Tribunal. Dinner at Gorbunov's.

To Vladimir, behind the same old nags. Heavy going, trackless mud, road impassable. We arrive in the night. Hassle over lodgings, a cold room in a widow's house. Jews—shopkeepers. Papa and mama—elderly people.

Are you grieving, grandma? Her gentle, black-bearded husband. A pregnant redheaded Jewish woman washes her feet. The little girl has diarrhea. It's cramped, but there's electricity, and it's warm.

Supper is dumplings with sunflower oil—bliss. This is it—Jewish plenty. They think I don't understand Yiddish, they're about as cunning as flies. The town is dirt-poor.

Borodin and I sleep on a feather bed.

9 September 1920. Vladimir-Volynskii

The town is dirt-poor, filthy, hungry, you can't buy anything with money, sweets twenty rubles apiece plus cigarettes. Feel wretched. Army HQ. Dreary. Council of trade unions, young Jews. Go around economic councils and T.U. commissions, feel wretched, the military make demands, behave like hooligans. Sickly young Jews.

Luxurious dinner—meat, kasha. Our only pleasure is food.

New military commissar at HQ—face like a monkey.

My hosts want to swap something for my shawl. I won't fall for it.

My driver—barefoot, with puffy eyes. Real Ru-u-ussia.

The synagogue. I pray, bare walls, some soldier goes around appropriating the light bulbs.

The bathhouse. Curse the soldiery, the war, the crowding together of young, tormented, wild, still healthy people.

The private life of my hosts, they go about their business, tomorrow is Friday, they're already preparing for it, the old woman is nice, the old man a bit crafty, they pretend to be poor. They say it's better to go hungry under the Bolsheviks than to eat fine bread under the Poles.

10 September 1920. Kovel

Half a day at the battered, dreary, horrible station in Vladimir-Volynsk. Misery. A black-bearded Jew working. We enter Kovel at night. Unexpected joy—the Army Political Education train. Supper with Zdanevich, butter. Spend the night in the radio station. Blinding light. Miracles. Khelemskaya is somebody's mistress. Lymphatic glands. Volodya. She stripped. My prophecy has come true.

11 September 1920. Kovel

The town retains traces of European-Jewish culture. They won't take Soviet money, a glass of coffee without sugar costs 50 rubles, a rotten meal at the station 600 rubles.

Sunshine, I go from one doctor to another, trying to get my ear treated, terrible itch.

Go to visit Yakovlev, quiet little houses, meadows, Jewish back streets, a quiet life, wholesome, Jewish girls, youths, old men by the synagogue, perhaps wigs, Soviet power doesn't seem to have troubled the surface, those parts of the town over the bridge.

The train is dirty and hungry. They're all emaciated, lousy, yellow in the face, all hate one another, sit locked in their compartments, even the cook has lost weight. A startling change. They live in a cage. Dirty Khelemskaya plays at cooking, contact with the kitchen, she feeds Volodya, a Jewish wife "from a good home."

I spend the whole day looking for food.

Area of deployment of the 12th Army. Luxurious establishments—clubs, gramophones, politically literate Red Army men, it's cheerful, the pulse of life beats strongly, the 12th Army's newspapers, Army HQ News Service, Army Commander Kuzmin, who writes articles, the Political Section's work seems to be well organized.

How the Jews live, crowds in the street, the main street is Lutsk Street, I walk around on my bruised feet, drink an immeasurable quantity of tea and coffee. Ice cream—500 rubles. They've got a lot of nerve. Saturday, all the shops closed. Medicine—5 rubles.

I spend the night at the radio station. Blinding light, smart-aleck radio operators, one of them trying to play a mandolin. They both read voraciously.

12 September 1920. Kivertsy

In the morning—panic at the railroad station. Artillery fire. The Poles are in the town. Unimaginably wretched flight, wagons five abreast, wretched, dirty, breathless infantrymen, cavemen, run off over the meadows, throw away their rifles, dispatch rider Borodin sees the Poles hacking us to bits already. The train moves out quickly, soldiers and wagons rush alongside, wounded men with distorted faces jump into our railroad car, a political officer, panting, his trousers fallen down, a Jew with a delicate, translucent face, perhaps a cunning Jew, deserters with broken arms jump on, sick men from the mobile infirmary.

The institution known as the 12th Army. For every fighting man there are 4 in the rear, 2 ladies, 2 trunks full of belongings, and that one fighting man isn't fighting anyway. The 12th Army is the ruin of the whole Army Group and of the Cavalry Army, it exposes our flanks, forces us to plug all the holes up ourselves. One of its units has surrendered, either a Ukrainian regiment or a Bashkir brigade, and left the front wide open. Shameful panic, an army incapable of fighting. Types of soldiers. The Russian Red Army infantryman, not just unmodernized, but the personification of "pauper Russia," wayfaring tramps, unhealthily swollen, bug-ridden, scrubby, half-starved peasants.

At Goloby the sick, the wounded, and the deserters are all thrown off the train. Rumors, afterward confirmed: the supply column of the 1st Cavalry Army, sent into the Vladimir-Volynsk cul-de-sac, has been seized by the enemy, our HQ has transferred to Lutsk, the 12th Army has lost a great number of men taken prisoner, a great deal of equipment, the whole army is on the run.

We arrive in Kivertsy in the evening.

Life on the train is an ordeal. The radio operators are always scheming to get rid of me, one of them still has an upset stomach, he plays the mandolin, the other makes clever remarks, because he's an idiot.

Railroad-car life, dirty, bad-tempered, hungry, a life of hostility to one another, unhealthy. Smoking, gorging Muscovites, look like nothing on earth, many pitiful people, coughing Muscovites, they're all hungry, all bad-tempered, all have stomach trouble.

13 September 1920. Kivertsy

Fine morning, forest. The Jewish New Year. Hungry. I walk into the town. Little boys in white collars. An *eshes chayil* treats me to bread and butter. She has to "support myself," a tough woman, silk dress, house tidy. I was moved to tears, only language could help here, we talk at length, her husband is in America, a sensible, steady Jewish woman.

Long wait in the station. The usual tedium. We borrow books from the club, read voraciously.

14 September 1920. Klevan

We wait 24 hours in Klevan, the whole time at the station. Hunger, tedium. Rovno won't take us. A railroad worker. We bake biscuits and potatoes in his shack. Railroad watchman. They eat dinner, say kind words, give us nothing. I'm with Borodin, his light-footed walk. We spend the whole day trying to get food, from one watchman's hut to another. Spend the night in the radio station under blinding light.

15 September 1920. Klevan

The third day of our excruciating halt in Klevan is beginning, the same old walk-around for food, this morning we drank a lot of tea, with flatcakes. In the evening I went to Rovno, on a cart belonging to the 1st Cavalry Army's air support. Conversation about our air force, nonexistent, all the machines damaged, the airmen haven't learnt to fly properly, the aircraft are old, patched up, no use at all. The Red Army man with the bad throat—now there's a type. He can hardly speak, his throat is probably blocked, inflamed, he pokes his finger in to scratch the mucus from his throat, people had told him salt helps, he sprinkles salt into it, hasn't eaten for four days, drinks cold water because nobody gives him any hot. Speaks in a thick voice about the attack, the commander, the fact that they were all barefoot, some advance, others don't, he gestures with his finger.

Supper at Gasnikova's.

THE DIARY BREAKS OFF AT THIS POINT.

Appendix: Babel's Publications in the *Red Cavalryman*

Babel wrote for the First Cavalry Army newspaper *Krasnyi kavalerist* [the *Red Cavalryman*] under the bylines K.L. or K. Lyutov. Although the following articles and the letter to the editor are the only items in the paper with his byline, he presumably wrote other pieces as well. His letter to the editor indicates the difficulties of the correspondent's situation: he was often isolated from printed news sources and did not know whether his dispatches were getting through.

A comparison of Babel's articles with others in the paper, on the one hand, and with his diary entries and later stories, on the other, makes clear how in some respects Babel geared his journalistic writing to the sort of propagandistic hyperbole typical of this and other military newspapers. The accounts of anti-Semitic atrocities in Berestechko ("Knights of Civilization") and Komarów ("The Killers Must Be Finished Off"), and of the ordeals of a nurse under fire ("Her Day"), however, bear similarities to the style and substance of the diary entries.

13 August 1920
We Need More Trunovs!

To our heroic, bloody, and sorrowful record one more name must be added, a name unforgettable for the 6th Division, that of Konstantin Trunov, commander of the 34th Cavalry Regiment, who was killed in battle at K. on 3 August. Yet another grave will lie hidden in the shade of the dense Volhynian forests, yet another notable life, full of self-sacrifice and loyalty to duty, has been laid down for the cause of the oppressed, yet another proletarian heart has been shattered, to dye the red banners of revolution with its own hot blood. The history of Comrade Trunov's last years is inseparably bound up with the titanic struggle of the Red Army. He drank the cup to the dregs, took part in every campaign from Tsaritsyn to Voronezh, and from Voronezh to the shores of the Black Sea. His past was one of hunger, privation, wounds, fighting against odds, foremost among the first ranks, until at last a bullet from a Polish Pan and officer cut down the peasant from the far-off steppes of Stavropol who had brought to people foreign to him the tidings of liberation.

From the first days of the Revolution, never wavering for a minute, Comrade Trunov occupied his proper place. We found him among the organizers of the first contingents from Stavropol. In the regular Red Army he occupied successively the posts of commander of the 4th Stavropol Regiment, commander of the 1st Brigade of the 32nd Division, and commander of the 34th Cavalry Regiment of the 6th Division.

His memory will not fade in the ranks of our fighting men. In the most difficult circumstances he wrested victory from the enemy by his exceptional and unreserved bravery, his steadfast determination, the cool composure that never deserted him, and his enormous influence on the Red Army masses who were his kith and kin. Let us have more Trunovs—and put an end to all the world's Pans.

Military Correspondent of the 6th Cavalry Division K. Lyutov

14 August 1920
Knights of Civilization

The Polish army has gone berserk. Mortally stung, at their last gasp, the Pans are rushing about in their death throes, heaping crime on stupidity, descending ignominiously into the grave to the curses of their own people as well as others. Feeling as they had before, they charge ahead wildly, careless of the future, completely forgetting that their Entente governesses think of them as knights of European civilization, the guardians of "law and order," and a barrier against Bolshevik barbarism.

This is how the Polish barrier safeguards civilization.

There once lived in Berestechko a humble worker, a pharmacist who had organized a vital service: he never took a moment's rest from his patients, his test tubes and prescriptions—and he had nothing at all to do with politics and may very well have thought that Bolsheviks had ears above their eyes.

This pharmacist was a Jew. To a Pole that says it all: dumb beasts who can't answer back, why waste bullets—cut them up, rape them, torture them. In the twinkling of an eye they prepared a demonstration. The harmless pharmacist, who had succeeded in contracting piles sitting over his medicine bottles, was accused of having somewhere, sometime, for some reason killed a Polish officer, which meant that he was an accomplice of the Bolsheviks.

What followed takes us back to the most stifling age of the Spanish Inquisition. If I had not seen with my own eyes that tortured face, that mangled and mutilated body, I would never have believed that anything so extraordinarily wicked was possible anywhere in our times, cruel and bloody as they are. They branded the pharmacist's body with red-hot irons, burning stripes like those on a cavalryman's breeches into his flesh (as much as to say, "You're in league with those Bolshevik Cossacks"), they drove red-hot needles under his nails, they cut a Red Army star into his chest, they pulled out the hairs from his head, one by one.

All this was done without any hurry, and to the accompaniment of jokes at the expense of communism and Yid commissars.

This was not all—the Pans, insane with rage, razed the pharmacy to the ground, trampled all the medicines under foot, left not so much as one little packet untouched, and so the town is abandoned to its fate without medical aid. You won't even find a powder for a toothache in Berestechko. Its population of 20,000 is left to the ravages of epidemics and disease.

Behold the death throes of the szlachta. Behold the vicious, rabid dog at his last gasp. Finish him off, Red warriors, finish him off whatever the cost—now, today! There is not a moment to lose.

K.L.

11 September 1920
To the Editor of the *Red Cavalryman*

Dear Comrade Zdanevich:

The uninterrupted fighting of the past month has thrown us out of gear.

We live in trying circumstances—endless marches and counter-marches, advances, retreats. We are cut off completely from what is called civilized life. For the past month we have not seen a single newspaper; as for what is going on in the world at large, we have no idea. We could be living in a forest. In fact that's what we are doing—the forests are the scene of our wanderings.

I do not know whether my reports are getting through. Such conditions can make one despair. Among soldiers living in complete ignorance of what is going on, you get the most absurd rumors. This does incalculable harm. Urgent measures must be taken to supply the 6th Division, our largest, with our own papers and those from other towns.

For me personally I beg you to do the following: instruct the dispatchers: 1) to send me at least a three-week run of the newspaper, and include with it all the available papers from other towns; 2) to send daily at least 5 copies of our paper to me at the following address: HQ 6th Division, War Correspondent K. Lyutov. This is absolutely essential in order for me to get oriented.

How are things at the editorial office? It has not been possible for my work to proceed at all smoothly. We are totally exhausted. Some weeks you could not snatch as much as a half hour to write a few words.

I hope it will now be possible to start doing things in a more orderly fashion.

Write and let me know your intentions, plans, and requirements, so as to keep me in contact with the outside world.

With comradely greetings,
K. Lyutov

17 September 1920
The Killers Must Be Finished Off

They avenged themselves for what the workers did in 1905. They joined in punitive expeditions to shoot and strangle our benighted servile villages, which had briefly felt the breath of freedom on their faces.

In October 1917 they tore off their masks and marched with fire and sword against the Russian proletariat. For almost three years they tortured a country already tortured beyond endurance. We had thought that they were finished. We left them to die a natural death, but they had no intention of doing so.

Now we are paying for our mistakes. The illustrious Wrangel struts about the Crimea like a pouter pigeon, and the pathetic remnants of the Russian Black Hundred gangs who fought with Denikin have now turned up among the ultracivilized troops of their High-and-Mightinesses the Polish Pans. This riffraff, which has so far escaped the sword, has rallied to the Polish counts, the Potockis and Taraszczyckis, to save civilization and the rule of law from the barbarians. Let me tell you how civilization had been saved in Komarów, which was occupied on 28 August by units of the 6th Cavalry Division.

The Cossack captain Yakovlev's brave lads had been in town the night before—that same Yakovlev who offered us a sweet and peaceful life in our own Cossack villages, carpeted with the corpses of commissars, Yids, and Red Army soldiers.

As our squadrons drew near these Knights dispersed like smoke. But not before they had accomplished what they were there to do.

We found the Jewish population robbed of all they had, hacked to death, severely wounded. Our soldiers, who have seen a thing or two, and cut off a head or two themselves, recoiled in horror from the picture that met their eyes. The wretched hovels had been left in ruins, and inside, naked seventy-year-old men with their skulls bashed in and tiny children with their fingers hacked off, many of them still alive, wallowed in pools of blood, and raped old women, their bellies slit open, lay hunched up in corners with wild looks of unendurable despair frozen on their faces. The living crept about among the dead, stumbling over mangled corpses, staining their hands and faces in sticky, evil-smelling blood, afraid to venture out of their houses, thinking that it was not yet over.

Along the streets of the benumbed town wandered cringing, frightened shadows, trembling at the sound of a human voice, wailing for mercy whenever they were hailed. We came across apartments shrouded in eerie silence—an old grandfather lying there with all his family beside him. Father, grandchildren—all in contorted, unhuman poses.

Altogether, more than 30 people had been killed and about 60 injured. Two hundred women had been raped, and many of them done to death. Women had jumped from second or third stories, and broken arms or heads, trying to escape from the rapists. Our medical services worked all day without a break and still could not fully satisfy the need for help. The horrors of the Middle Ages pale in comparison with the bestial cruelties of Yakovlev's bandits.

The pogrom was, of course, carried out strictly in accordance with regulations. The officers began by demanding that the Jewish population purchase their safety for 50 thousand rubles. The money, and vodka, were immediately forthcoming, in spite of which the officers were in the first ranks when the pogroms began, zealously searching for bombs and machine guns in the houses of mortally terrified old Jews.

This is our reply to howls from the Polish Red Cross about Russian atrocities. This is one fact among a thousand more terrible facts.

The dogs whom we have still to put down have let out their hoarse yelp. The murderers who await the final blow have crawled out of their coffins.

Soldiers of the Red Army, finish them off! Beat down harder on the opening covers of their stinking graves!

Military Correspondent of the 6th Cavalry Division K. Lyutov

18 September 1920
Her Day

I had a sore throat. I went to see the nurse at the First HQ Squadron, N. Division. A smoky cottage, full of fumes and foul smells. Soldiers lolled around on benches, smoking, scratching themselves, and swearing. The nurse had taken refuge in a corner. Quietly and without unnecessary fuss she was bandaging the wounded one after another. Some mischievous ones did all they could to make it difficult. They all showed great ingenuity in the most unnatural and blasphemous abuse. While I was there the alarm was sounded, and the order came—"To horse." The squadron formed up. We were moving out.

The nurse bridled her horse herself, tied its feed bag on, collected her bundle, and rode off. Her pathetically flimsy dress flapped in the wind, you could see her frozen red toes through the holes in her worn-out shoes. It was raining. The exhausted horses could scarcely drag their hooves out of that terrible, squelchy, clinging Volhynian mud. The damp penetrated to your bones. The nurse had neither waterproof cape nor greatcoat. Men near to her struck up an obscene song. The nurse began singing a little song of her own under her breath—about dying for the Revolution, about the better future awaiting us. First one, then another of the men joined in, and our song streamed out into the rainy autumn twilight, our irrepressible call to freedom.

In the evening came the attack. Shells bursting with a sinister, soft sound, machine guns chattering ever more quickly, with feverish anxiety.

When the bombardment was at its most horrific the nurse, coolly contemptuous of it, went on bandaging the wounded, dragging them from the battlefield on her back.

The attack ended. Another agonizing ride. Night, rain. The soldiers were morosely silent, and the only sound was the nurse's warmhearted whispering as she comforted the wounded. An hour later it was the usual picture—dark, dirty cottage, in which a platoon had billeted itself, and the nurse in a corner, lit by a miserable candle-end, bandaging, bandaging, bandaging . . .

The air was thick with foul language. Occasionally, when she could stand it no longer, the nurse would snap at them, and they would laugh and laugh at her. There was no one to help her, no one to make her a bed of straw for the night, no one to smooth her pillow.

That is what they are like, our heroic nurses! Caps off to our nurses! Soldiers and commanders, show respect to our nurses. It is high time we started distinguishing between the camp followers who disgrace our army, and the martyr nurses who adorn it.

K. Lyutov

Notes

People: For the identification of many individuals mentioned by Babel, I am indebted to the notes prepared by S. N. Povartsov for the Russian edition of the diary, Isaak Babel', *Sochineniia,* 2 vols. (Moscow: Khudozhestvennaia literatura, 1990), v. 1, and to the superb German edition translated and annotated by Peter Urban, Isaak Babel, *Tagebuch 1920* (Berlin: Friedenauer Presse, 1990). In many cases, however, full identification is not available.

Places: Much could be written about the towns through which Babel passed; most, however, can be looked up in standard sources. In order to give readers a sense of scale and at least a sketchy feel for the setting, I have included a brief description of some towns, with population figures circa 1920. Figures for the towns within the borders of interwar Poland are taken from Bohdan Wasiutyński, *Ludność żydowska v Polsce w wiekach XIX i XX* (Warsaw: Instytut popierania nauki, 1930). For places that came to be part of the USSR, I have used that country's 1926 census, *Vsesoiuznaia perepis' naseleniia* (Moscow: Tsentral'noe statisticheskoe upravlenie, 1927–29). Figures from the previous census (1897) are used only for a few small towns that could not be located in sources closer to 1920; the figures are taken from the *Entsiklopedicheskii slovar',* 41 vols. (St. Petersburg:

Brockhaus-Efron, 1890–1904). As with the people, full identification is not always available.

The Diary and Babel's Stories: Readers familiar with the *Red Cavalry* stories will recognize in these entries many individuals, incidents, and bits of realia. I have refrained from noting every correspondence but have indicated major instances. Correspondences of mood and language (at least as important as those of incident and character, if not more so) are too frequent to cite. As my Introduction indicates, the stories also depart from the diary in important respects.

1920 Diary

3 June [July]

Date: Babel probably slipped in noting this date as well as those of the three entries dated June that follow. Norman Davies, in "Izaak Babel"s 'Konarmiya' Stories, and the Polish-Soviet War" (*Modern Language Review* 67, no. 4 [October 1972]: 847), points out that Babel could not have been in Zhitomir on 3 June because Zhitomir and other nearby towns passed through in the "June" entries were then still held by the Poles. While sources differ on which day the Reds took Zhitomir, the earliest date given for the Soviet occupation is 9 June. Davies suggests that Babel might have meant to write "July," which is plausible, given that in the Roman numerals he used to denote months, six and seven differ by only one stroke. Efraim Sicher argues in support of this view, noting also that the first entry describes a Saturday, and 3 July (unlike 3 June) fell that year on a Saturday. See his "The 'Jewish Cossack': Isaac Babel in the First Red Cavalry," *Studies in Contemporary Jewry* 4 (1988): 113–34.

Zhitomir: Pop. 68,280 (1926); ethnic makeup at that time, 39.2 percent Jews, 37.1 percent Ukrainians, 13.7 percent Russians, 7.4 percent Poles. In the second half of the nineteenth century, site of a rabbinical seminary and an important center of Hebrew publishing and Jewish intellectual life. The city is eighty-three miles west-southwest of Kiev, where Babel had studied from 1911 to 1914, and thus not so distant from familiar territory.

Morning in the train: This was a train of what in Soviet military acronymese was called the *Poarm*—the Political Section of the army. Equipped for the mission of carrying on political education among soldiers and civilians, it had (among other things) a printing shop and editorial office, a radio station, and (as the end of the entry makes clear) a film projector. Babel describes leaving the train in the third entry and rejoins it on 10 September.

Zhukov, Topolnik: Fellow correspondents for the *Red Cavalryman.*

Yugrosta: Southern branch of the national wire service, ROSTA (acronym of Rossiiskoe telegrafnoe agentstvo), for which Babel was working as a correspondent for the troop newspaper the *Red Cavalryman.*

Pollak: Staff officer of the Sixth Division.

Love in the kitchen: A theme treated in "Evening," a *Red Cavalry* story that conveys the atmosphere in and around one of those train kitchens at the end of the day.

A little Jew, a philosopher: See Babel's treatment of the man, his shop, and his words in the *Red Cavalry* story "Gedali."

Budyonny, Semyon Mikhailovich (1883–1973): Founder (in 1919) and commander of the First Cavalry Army; played an important role in defeating the Whites in the Civil War. Subsequently promoted to the rank of marshal and made a member of the Central Committee; named first deputy commissar for defense in 1940 (under Voroshilov, with whom we see him in several diary entries).

Zhitomir pogrom: The pogrom referred to had occurred during the Polish occupation of the city and continued after the Soviets took control, presumably a few weeks before Babel arrived (see note on date above). Babel would have known that Zhitomir, which changed hands a number of times during the Civil War years, had also suffered two large-scale pogroms in 1919 (7–10 January and 22–26 March) while it was held by Ukrainian nationalist troops.

tsaddik: A Hasidic leader recognized for his spiritual guidance and wisdom. The scene is reflected (far from precisely) in Babel's stories "The Rebbe" and "The Rebbe's Son."

4 June [July]

Narbut, Vladimir Ivanovich (1888–1944): From 1920 to 1922, director of YugROSTA in Odessa.

Khelemskaya: Apparently another member of the staff of the political division. Babel scrutinizes her again when he rejoins the train on 10 September.

5 June [July]

Novograd: Also called Novograd-Volynsk; Polish name Zwiahel (Babel refers to this other name at the end of the first paragraph). Pop. 14,433 (1926). Taken by the First Cavalry Army on 27 June. Babel just passes through Novograd here, but four of the stories in *Red Cavalry* are set there: "Crossing into Poland," "The Church at Novograd," "Pan Apolek," and "Italian Sunshine."

Thornycroft: A British-made car, probably one of the military models used in World War I. The British had supplied the Whites in the Civil War, including the Volunteer Army commanded by General Denikin, with a large amount of military hardware. The troops of *Denikin, Anton Ivanovich* (1872–1947), were defeated in the Kuban region in March 1920 by Red troops including Budyonny's First Cavalry Army, which then began its march toward the Polish front.

Korets: Pop. 4,946 (1921); 79 percent Jews.

yeshiva bocher: Student of a rabbinical academy (Yiddish).

versts: The old Russian measure of one *versta* equals 1.06 kilometers.

Hoszcza: Pop. 2,091 (1897); about 45 percent Jews.

Zotov, S. A. (1882–1938): Field staff commander of the Sixth Division.

Duvid Uchenik: The surname means "student" or "disciple" in Russian.

Horyn: River that flows through Hoszcza.

Belaya Tserkov: Town in the Ukraine, south of Kiev. Babel is apparently alluding in this sentence to a story he told to reinforce his incomplete truth that he was Jewish on his mother's side. It was true that his paternal grandfather had pursued rabbinical studies. One wonders whether his account of his heritage was similar to the one he gives his narrator in "The Story of My Dovecot" (1925)—a story that gives the illusion of autobiography but is not: "My grandfather had been a rabbi somewhere in the Belaya Tserkov region. He had been thrown out for blasphemy, and for another forty years he lived noisily and sparsely, teaching foreign languages" (*The Collected Stories*, trans. Walter Morison [New York: World, 1972], 255).

6 June [July]

Rovno: Pop. 30,842 (1921); 71 percent Jews. In the nineteenth century became a commercial center dealing in military supplies; after the completion of the Kiev-Warsaw and Vilna-Rovno railroads late in the century, it was an important rail junction and also a center of Zionism and Hebrew education. In the spring of 1919 pogroms were perpetrated in Rovno by Ukrainian troops loyal to Ukrainian nationalist leader Simon Petlyura.

tallis: Prayer shawl (Yiddish).

11 July

Belyov: Village about 15 kilometers northwest of Rovno.

manuscripts: Apparently some writing on which Babel had been working and which had been lost.

Klevan: Pop. 3,739 (1897); about 65 percent Jews.

Dundich, Oleko (1893–1920): Aide to the commander of the 36th Cavalry Regiment of the Sixth Division.

tachanka: A kind of horse-drawn buggy, turned to military purpose by mounting a machine gun on it. A detailed and rhapsodic description can be found in Babel's story "Discourse on the *Tachanka.*"

Schossowa: Babel writes this in Latin characters; it is a Germanized spelling of the Polish adjective *szosowa* (highroad).

note to Wilson: It is unclear precisely what diplomatic message is referred to, though presumably it was one sent to Woodrow Wilson by the Soviet government. Possibly this had to do with the U.S. announcement on 7 July that all restrictions against communications and trade (except for military-related material) with Soviet Russia had been removed. The same announcement emphasized that recognition of the new government would continue to be withheld.

labor armies: The Ninth Congress of the Communist Party, meeting in March–April 1920, had approved as part of the transition to peacetime a plan (vigorously promoted by Trotsky) of mass labor conscription, which was organized along the lines of military conscription.

pre-Reform times: The reference is to the period before 1861, when major social and economic reforms, including the emancipation of the serfs, were instituted by Alexander II.

Brusilov, Aleksei Alekseevich (1853–1926): Russian general; as commander of the southwest sector of the eastern front in World War I, responsible for the "Brusilov breakthrough" of June–August 1916, in which Russian troops pushed back Austro-Hungarian forces in Bukovina and eastern Galicia. Stirred by the Polish invasion to offer his services to the

Red Army and to urge other former tsarist officers to do the same, Brusilov served from 1920 to 1924 as military adviser and inspector of cavalry.

Zholnarkevich, Konstantin Karlovich: Staff commander of the Sixth Division. The brother referred to was a staff officer as well. Usually referred to by Babel as "Konstantin Karlovich" or "K. Karlych."

13 July

Dyakov: See Babel's story "The Remount Officer" for another portrait of Dyakov. Elements of the entries for 14 and 16 July that deal with taking horses from the local population are also reflected in the story.

14 July

Frank Mosher: This was an alias used by Captain Merian C. Cooper of Jacksonville, Florida, whose idea it was to form the Kosciuszko Squadron, a unit of pilots, principally American, who fought on the Polish side. The squadron was under the command of *Cedric E. Fauntleroy,* mentioned in this and several other entries. After serving as a pilot in World War I, Cooper had worked for the American Relief Administration in southern Poland. By Cooper's account, the name Frank Mosher was stenciled on the army surplus underwear he had been issued, and he used it to protect his real identity, insisting that he was a worker who had been conscripted. (Babel was correct in suspecting that Mosher was feigning interest in Bolshevism.) After months in Soviet prisons Mosher escaped and, in April 1921, made his way to Riga. See Robert F. Karolevitz and Ross S. Fenn, *Flight of Eagles: The Story of the American Kosciuszko Squadron in the Polish-Russian War 1919–1920* (Sioux Falls, S.D.: Brevet, 1974), and the memoir by Kenneth Malcolm Murray, *Wings over Poland* (New York: D. Appleton, 1932). Cooper's own memoir, *Things Men Die For* (New York: Putnam, 1927), published under the pseudonym "C," has vignettes of his experiences in Poland and as a Soviet prisoner. His love of books and good command of French (the language in which he and Babel probably conversed) are described there (one book for which he bartered a pair of shoes while a prisoner was Zola's *Nana*), but there is nothing about his capture by the First Cavalry Army or about a character resembling Babel.

Grishchuk: Depicted in the stories "The Death of Dolgushov" and "Discourse on the *Tachanka.*"

Timoshenko, Semyon Konstantinovich (1895–1970): Commander of the Sixth Division until early August. Savitsky in *Red Cavalry* ("My First Goose," "The Story of a Horse," and other stories) appears to be modeled on him.

Kniga, V. I. (1882–1961): Commander of the First Brigade of the Sixth Division.

15 July

Bakhturov, P. V. (1889–1920): Military commissar (chief political officer) of the Sixth Division from November 1919 to August 1920.

Piłsudski, Józef (1867–1935): President of Poland and commander in chief of the Polish Army, 1918–1922. Served as minister of defense and continued to be the major influence on political policy from 1926 until his death.

Rzecz pospolita: Republic (Polish).

18 July

Khmelnitsky, Bogdan (c. 1595–1657): As leader of the Zaporozhian Cossacks, led a rebellion against Polish rule in Ukraine that brought about the transfer of the region east of the Dnepr River from Polish to Russian control. The reference here is to the massacre of many Jews by Khmelnitsky's Cossacks.

Karl Karlovich: A slip; Babel apparently means *Konstantin* Karlovich (Zholnarkevich), the staff commander.

19 July

Kolesov, N. P.: Commander of one of the regiments of the Sixth Division.

Voroshilov, Kliment Efremovich (1881–1969): At this time, commissar of the First Cavalry Army and member of its Revolutionary Military Council; headed the Red Army 1925–1940.

20 July

Starting with this entry and consistently until the end of the diary (with the exception of 27 July), Babel reverses the order of his heading, writing first the date, then the place. For a number of dates after late July no location is given, presumably because Babel was so much on the move and not always in or near a town when he wrote.

21 July

Kozin: Pop. 1,820 (1897); 50 percent Jews. Babel gives a terse and dramatic depiction of the cemetery in his story "The Cemetery at Kozin."

jovial: Babel (who knew French well) uses the French word.

23 July

Verba: The *Red Cavalry* story "Two Ivans" has a description of entering Verba.

Dubno: Pop. 9,146 (1921); 58 percent Jews. For centuries, Dubno had one of the oldest and most important Jewish communities in eastern Europe.

pood: The Russian measure of one pood equals 16.3 kilograms.

Prishchepa: See the *Red Cavalry* story translated as "Prishchepa's Vengeance," which gives a version of the story Prishchepa recounts in the entry for 24 July.

a grober mensch: A boor (Yiddish).

er ist ein: "He's a . . . ." (German). The illegible word that follows may refer to Babel's being a Jew.

Hershele: A trickster from Yiddish folklore; Babel had written one story about him ("Shabbos-Nachamu," 1918) and planned a cycle of Hershele stories (apparently never written).

24 July

Demidovka: Pop. 679 (1897); all Jews.

Kadets: Members of the Constitutional Democratic Party, a liberal pre-Revolutionary party that opposed Bolshevism; used here as a loose reference to soldiers fighting on the side of the Whites.

Artsybashev, Mikhail Petrovich (1878–1927): Russian writer known for his Nietzsche-influenced novels dealing with free love, violence, and the gratification of individual desires; popular (and controversial), especially for the novel *Sanin* (1907).

9th of Av: The ninth day of the Hebrew month of Av, usually referred to in English (by its Hebrew name) as Tisha b'Av. This holiday is a day of fasting and mourning, commemorating the destruction of the two Temples in Jerusalem that were the center of Jewish religious life: the First (destroyed by the Babylonians in 586 B.C.) and the Second (destroyed by the Romans in A.D. 70). Babel arrives at the dentist's home on Saturday toward evening—that is, toward the end of the Sabbath, on which observant Jews like these must refrain from all activities defined as work, including the preparation of food. The Sabbath would not be over until sundown (which comes late at this time of year), and at sundown the fast of Tisha b'Av would begin.

In the synagogue on Tisha b'Av, as signs of mourning, benches are turned over and the curtain over the Ark where the Torah is kept is removed. Traditional practice requires that all sit either on the floor or on overturned benches—that explains why Babel describes the old woman of the household as sitting on the floor. The text her son chants is from Lamentations, the central liturgy for the holiday. The phrases Babel gives allude to passages from Lamentations. "They eat dung" may be a reference to Lamentations 4:5: "They that did feed on dainties / Are desolate in the streets; / They that were brought up in scarlet / Embrace dunghills." "Their maidens are ravished, their menfolk killed" may be shorthand for the lines in 5:11–13: "They have ravished the women in Zion, / The maidens in the cities of Judah. / Princes are hanged up by their hand; / The faces of the elders are not honoured." Another passage Babel would have heard if Lamentations were recited in its entirety helps one understand his perception of an analogy between past and present. It is 5:1–3: "Remember, O Lord, what is come upon us; / Behold, and see our reproach. / Our inheritance is turned unto strangers, / Our houses unto aliens."

Platonov, Sergei Fedorovich (1860–1933): The leading Russian historian of his day.

Perun: In Slavic mythology, the god of thunder.

story of the Chinese: Perhaps an anecdote similar to the story Babel published in 1923 (translated as "The Chinaman"), which involves a Chinese man and a prostitute in post-Revolutionary Petrograd. The theme was evidently one that particularly caught his imagination: Viktor Shklovsky, describing Babel as he was in 1919, joked that he "wrote little, but steadily. It was always the same story—about two Chinamen in a brothel. . . . A good many stories resulted from all this, and not just one." ("Isaac Babel: A Critical Romance," trans. John Pearson, in *Modern Critical Views: Isaac Babel,* ed. Harold Bloom [New Haven, Conn.: Chelsea House, 1987], p. 11.)

25 July

Leszniów: Pop. 1,871 (1921); about 10 percent Jews.

Plevitksaya, Nadezhda Vasilievna (1884–1941): Russian popular singer; emigrated 1920. Tried and convicted in 1938 in Paris for being a Soviet agent and for having helped her husband, General Skoblin, to abduct the head of the All-Russian Military Union in Paris, General Evgeny Miller.

26 July

Wrangel, Pyotr Nikolaevich (1878–1928): Russian general who in April 1920 succeeded Denikin as commander of the White armies after they had been forced to retreat to the Crimea.

Makhno, Nestor Ivanovich (1886–1934): Peasant leader of the anarchist movement in Ukraine; fought against the Whites but resisted subordination to Red Army control.

Brody: Pop. 10,867 (1921); 66 percent Jews. See also the entries for 30–31 July. A center of the Berlin Enlightenment (Haskalah) movement in Galicia. Important also in the nineteenth century in its role as an Austro-Hungarian border town; served as the first destination of many Russian Jews fleeing pogroms. In *Red Cavalry,* see "The Road to Brody."

Radziwiłłów (after 1940, Chervonoarmeisk): Pop. 4,240 (1921); 48 percent Jews.

27 July

armistice talks begin on the 30th: Talks had, in fact, been planned for 30 July; on 1 August in the town of Baranowicze, Polish and Russian delegations exchanged notes, but their negotiations came to nothing. (Piotr S.

Wandycz, *Soviet-Polish Relations, 1917–1921* [Cambridge: Harvard University Press, 1969], pp. 232–33.)

28 July

Zhenya: Babel's wife Evgenia (Zhenya for short), then in Odessa.

30 July

peyes: sidelocks worn by Orthodox Jewish males (Yiddish).

shammes: synagogue sexton (Yiddish). The *shammes* served primarily as a caretaker, but also might function as a notary, clerk, leader of prayer, or collector of charity.

31 July

the history of all the Boleslaws: a history of the Polish royal dynasty that ruled from 992 until the thirteenth century.

Tetmajer, Casimir (1865–1940): Polish novelist and poet.

Kostroma: Provincial town on the Volga northeast of Moscow.

1 August

Grzymałówka: Pop. 2,748 (1921); 54 percent Jews.

Mikhail Karlovich: The brother of Konstantin Karlovich Zholnarkevich (see note to 11 July, above).

Third International: The Second Congress of the Third International took place in Petrograd 19 July–7 August. In "My First Goose" Babel describes the narrator of *Red Cavalry* reading to the Cossacks a speech of Lenin's to the Congress; the commissar Vinogradov makes a speech about the Congress in "Berestechko."

2 August

aeroplane: In keeping with Babel's usage (here and throughout, he uses the archaic Russian *aeroplan* rather than the modern *samolyot*), the old-fashioned form of *airplane* has been retained.

Korochaev, D. D.: Served temporarily as division commander. Vividly described in the opening of "The Death of Dolgushov."

3 August

Kolesnikov: Brigade commander in the Third Division. The incident with Budyonny threatening Kolesnikov is used by Babel in his story "The Brigade Commander."

forest of Murom: Proverbial for a deep, dark forest.

An apiary, we search the hives: On destroying beehives, see "The Road to Brody"; more on this in the entry for 31 August.

4 August

Sheko, Ia. B.: From the beginning of August, staff commander of the Sixth Division, under *Apanasenko, Iosif Rodionovich* (1890–1943), who was commander of the Sixth Division from early August until October, replacing Timoshenko. Apanasenko was the model for Babel's *Red Cavalry* character Pavlichenko, who tells his story in "The Life and Adventures of Matthew Pavlichenko." See entry for 12 August, in which Babel makes a note to write Apanasenko's biography.

Comrade Khmelnitsky: R. P. Khmelnitsky, an adjutant of Voroshilov's.

6 August

they helped themselves to it in Rostov: Rostov-on-Don, fiercely contested in the Civil War, had been captured by the First Cavalry Army on 8 January 1920. The soldiers were reprimanded (and a number prosecuted) for looting and for violence directed against civilians.

7 August

Berestechko: Pop. 5,633 (1921); 35 percent Jews. *Historic fields outside Berestechko* (paragraph four) refers to the battle that took place 28–30 June 1651, in which Cossack and Tatar troops fighting under Bogdan Khmelnitsky were defeated by the Polish Army. In *Red Cavalry*, see "Berestechko" and "In St. Valentine's Church." Babel also wrote a piece for the *Red*

Cavalryman on Polish atrocities in the town, entitled "Knights of Civilization" (see Appendix).

Hauptmann; Elga: The German writer Gerhardt Hauptmann (1862–1946) wrote in 1896 a play called *Elga* (based on a novella by Franz Grillparzer), set in a Polish monastery.

Revolutionary Committee: The division Political Department was responsible for arranging the formation, in each locale under Red control, of a local governing body (*revkom* in Russian) to serve as a temporary organ of martial law.

rising in India: A reference to the campaign against the British led by Gandhi, who had set 1 August 1920 as a day of fasting and prayer that would launch his *satyagraha* movement.

m'shores: Servant (Yiddish).

8 August

Everybody's Magazine: The *Zhurnal dlia vsekh* was a popular illustrated periodical published in St. Petersburg from 1896 to 1909.

ataman: A Cossack leader (sometimes rendered *hetman*).

9 August

an epic conversation: A similar conversation takes place in the *Red Cavalry* story "The Letter."

Kuban Cossacks: Cossacks from the Kuban region; the second largest community of Cossacks after the Don Cossacks.

10 August

Chet'i-Minei: A Russian Orthodox menology (compilation of saints' lives and other writings organized according to months and saints' days—the term in Old Church Slavonic means "monthly readings") dating from the sixteenth century.

Szeptycki, Andrzej: Metropolitan of the Uniate Church in Galicia. The brother referred to, Stanisław, was a Polish general who played a major role in this war.

Vinokurov: A commissar; apparently Babel's model for the *Red Cavalry* character Vinogradov.

Dumenko, Boris Mokeevich (1888–1920): Cossack cavalry commander, Civil War hero.

11 August

Utochkin, S. I. (1896–1916): One of the first Russian pilots; born in Odessa.

George Crosses: Order of St. George, a medal in the tsarist army.

Shkuro and Mamontov: Cavalry commanders on the side of the Whites in the Civil War; fought under Denikin and Wrangel.

13 August

mowa: Language (Ukrainian).

15 August

Toporów: Pop. 3,421 (1921); 20 percent Jews.

18 August

Bebel, August (1840–1913): The reference in the next line is to the German socialist's *Women and Socialism* (1879).

Busk: Pop. 6,148 (1921); 25 percent Jews. The *Red Cavalry* story "The Widow" is set there.

prisoners: One of the *Red Cavalry* stories that deals with the treatment of Polish prisoners in ways resembling this entry is "Squadron Commander Trunov."

old or new Milatyn: The town names—Stary Milatyn and Nowy Milatyn—mean old and new Milatyn, respectively. They have been translated here to indicate the relation between them.

21 August

In Poland, where we're going: On 25 July Babel had crossed from Ukraine into Galicia, which had formerly been Austro-Hungarian but was newly Polish. The reference here is to moving north out of Galicia into what had been part of the Kingdom of Poland (within the Russian Empire) before World War I.

23–24 August

Witków: Pop. 2,176 (1921); 45 percent Jews.

25 August

Sokal: Pop. 10,183 (1921); 43 percent Jews. Between the two world wars, Zionism had considerable influence here.

angesprochener Nationalist: Babel (using the German apparently used by his interlocutor) means *ausgesprochener* (outspoken).

polnische, juden: In German in the original; literally, "Polish, Jews" (though Babel probably means the latter word as an adjective describing books he looked at, presumably in the household where he was lodged).

26 August

Rabbi of Bełz; Husiatyn rabbi: Bełz was the more important of the two Hasidic dynasties, and one of the most important in Galicia. The Rabbi of Bełz, Issachar Dov (1854–1927), had fled Galicia in 1914 to escape the war; he returned in 1921. (He is also mentioned in the entry for 9 August.) A description of the Hasidim in each camp is in the *Red Cavalry* story "Squadron Commander Trunov," set in Sokal.

The nurse—26 men and a girl: An allusion to Maxim Gorky's story "Twenty-Six Men and a Girl" (1899), in which a group of oppressed bakery workers adore and then abuse a young woman who, they feel, has betrayed their idea of her purity by sleeping with a soldier.

28 August

Komarów: Pop. 2,895 (1921); 60.5 percent Jews. Two accounts by survivors of the pogrom described here are included in a compendium of documents about violence against Jews during the Polish-Soviet War entitled *Inwazja Bolszewicka a Żydzi. Zbiór Dokumentów,* 2 vols. (Warsaw, 1921), vol. 2, pp. 20–21 and 104–06). The names of the dead listed by

Babel are documented here, although apparently Babel did not get all the names exactly right (both these accounts give two of the last names he records as Zysman—not Zys—and Zaler—not Galer). See Babel's account of the Komarów pogrom for the *Red Cavalryman* in the Appendix.

Captain Yakovlev's Cossacks: Yakovlev was a Cossack captain who went over to the Polish side. Babel vividly describes him and his brigade in the *Red Cavalry* story "After the Battle."

29 August

8,000 vedros: A *vedro* is equivalent to approximately 12 liters.

Operation to take Zamość: The unsuccessful Soviet effort to take Zamość (1921 pop. 24,241, about 40 percent Jews), a major center of Jewish intellectual life in the nineteenth century, is the focus of this entry and the next. The city, modeled on Padua by its founder Jan Zamoyski, was built as a walled fortress. The *Red Cavalry* story that bears the city's name conveys the rain and frustration suffered by the troops.

30 August

There were nine of them: This is the title Babel gave to a 1923 story that has its source at least in part in this incident. The story (not published in Babel's lifetime) has been translated into English as "And Then There Were None."

Putilov worker: The Putilov Works, founded 1801 in St. Petersburg (renamed the Red Putilovite in 1922; since 1934, the Kirov Works), was one of the largest metallurgical and machine-building enterprises in Russia, producing (among other things) locomotives, ships, and artillery. Putilov workers were active in the Revolutionary movement before 1917 and supported the Bolsheviks in the Civil War, producing weapons and armored trains for the Red Army.

31 August

Cześniki: A village 20 kilometers east of Zamość. The battle of 31 August, in which the Sixth Division lost all but four of its twenty squadron leaders (see Davies, *White Eagle, Red Star,* p. 231), considerably weakened the already weak First Cavalry Army and was "the only occasion in the war when two major cavalry forces confronted each other in mass formation. It was perhaps the last pure cavalry battle of European history" (p. 229). The *Red Cavalry* stories "Cześniki" and "After the Battle" reflect the experiences recounted in this entry and the next.

6 September

Budyatichi: This village is the setting of the *Red Cavalry* story "The Song."

8 September

Vladimir-Volynsk (also called Vladimir-Volynskii): Pop. 11,623 (1921); 94 percent Jews.

10 September

Kovel: Pop. 12,758 (1921); 61 percent Jews. A center of agricultural processing, sawmilling, clothing manufacture—and also a rail junction, which is significant here. Babel meets up in this entry with the train of the army's Political Section.

Zdanevich, V.: Editor of the *Red Cavalryman.* It is curious that Babel's letter of complaint to Zdanevich (see the Appendix) appeared in the newspaper (along with the editor's reply) the following day. Presumably both were written some time before the date of publication.

Khelemskaya: See notes to 4 June [July].

11 September

perhaps wigs: Wigs (the Yiddish term is *sheitel*) are worn by some pious Jewish married women as an emblem of modesty.

12 September

political officer, panting, his trousers fallen down: This retreat by rail figures in the *Red Cavalry* story "The Rebbe's Son," and the man described here calls to mind that story's protagonist.

13 September

eshes chayil: "A woman of valor" (Hebrew). From the poem in praise of the virtuous woman in Proverbs 31:10–31, which begins "A woman of valor who can find? / For her price is far above rubies."

14 September

Klevan: See notes to 11 July, when Babel passed through this town heading west. The First Cavalry Army was forced to retreat eastward after the defeat at Zamość. In the final entry, 15 September, Babel describes returning to Rovno (see notes to 6 June [July]).

Appendix

"We Need More Trunovs!"

For a fictionalized, disturbingly ambiguous portrait of the subject of this eulogy, see Babel's *Red Cavalry* story "Squadron Commander Trunov."

"Knights of Civilization"

See Babel's diary entries in Berestechko, 7–8 August.

Pan: A Polish honorific that can be used to mean "mister," "sir," or "gentleman" and that, in the plural, Babel uses to imply a contrast between bourgeois Poland and the new proletarian Russia.

szlachta: Gentry; also translated as "aristocracy" (Polish).

"The Killers Must Be Finished Off"

See the diary entry in Komarów, 28 August.